GREAT WORK, GREAT REWARDS

7 Secrets for Breaking the Performance Punishment Cycle

A self-help guide to reclaiming your joy when your ONLY reward for great work is more work

Liz Nolley Tillman

To Donna Marie,
You can do this!

To your success,

Liz Nolley Tillman

ISBN 978-1-5136-2212-5 (eBook edition)
ISBN 978-1-5136-2213-2 (print edition)

DISCLAIMER

DEDICATION

For all those who are brave enough to go beyond reaching for their brass rings and actually grabbing them. Always remember to celebrate the small victories along the way!

ACKNOWLEDGMENTS

Thanks to all of those who in some way helped or supported me in this journey to achieve my dream of becoming a published author, including: God for His perfect plan and for always lighting my path and guiding my steps; my family – Demetric, Mya, Shati, Jayden and Django – for their encouragement and support of my dream to become a published author; my Mom and Dad – Charles and Martha Nolley – the greatest parents and cheerleaders any kid could ask for; my brother – Rich Baraka – for always showing me what was possible through his example; my original and extended Sisterhood and Success circle – Ariane Newman, Kere Thomas, Nicole May-Bynes, Melodie Warner, Heather Williams, Sandra Lee, Toni Ross, Sonya Williams, Sonja Asante, Kim White, Pamela D. Smith-Robinson, Debra Witherspoon Perry-Kelly, Tanya Gardner, Leslie Faison, Michele Lamarre, Kiplyn Primus, Adrienne Montgomery and 'ma cousinne' and book cover designer Victoria Fleary – "I love ya'll like a fat kid loves cake" ☺; "Cousin" Stacey Smith Ragin and her mom, Carrie Barreiro and Jillian Rose for allowing God to wink at me through you; Coach Melinda Neisser, photographer Melody Meade, make-up artist and stylist Desiree Perrin, Lynda Slobodian, Neka Wilkerson-Blair and Scott Allan for using your gifts and talents to make me better; Owen Petrie, Al Orendorff, Mary Alice Horstman, Barry Hartsfield, my MKA teachers Mrs. Smith, Ms. Gerry and Mr. Noble, and my many other teachers, professors, colleagues, mentors and friends who have always encouraged me to write; Julia Diaz, Elona Gjiza and the rest of my QBR "dream team" and all those I've encountered in my professional journey for each experience and every lesson learned along the way; My Awesome Book Launch Team – Allan Dib, Alyson Beasley, Andrea Sawyer, Angela Booker Rodriguez, Colette Jackson, Francoise Neptune, Gene Booker, Holly Moore Johnson, Joe Polidoro, Kathy Thomas, Katherine Joyce, Maria Dolorico, Kirk Royster, Kurt Goldstein, Kyle Zekee, Lateefa Corum-Sadiq, Marcel Andre Green, Michelle Lee, Nicole Tomei Zwolinski, Rahman Sharif, Sandra Comarcho, Schania Davis, Tiffany Wellman, Vanessa Jenkins, Tammy Shaw-Rodano and Daphne Hill – for your ongoing cheers and support in getting me across the finish line; the Self Publishing School community for generously sharing your wisdom; and my wonderfully supportive sorority sisters of Alpha Kappa Alpha Sorority, Inc., especially the ITC 2014 - 2018 (Theresa House, Gwen Kimble, Anjelious Farmer, Jamela Wintons, Wendye Mingo, Shaliah Thierry, Tasha Roberts, Towanda Davila-Davis and Yvette Mitchell) and the Theta Kappa, Nu Xi Omega and Phi Eta Omega chapters. There are so many I wish to thank so if I've missed anyone, please charge it to my head, not my heart.

TABLE OF CONTENTS

Introduction – Why Are We Here? 9

Section 1 – How To Identify Performance Punishment **19**

Chapter 1 – Performance Punishment: The "King James" Version 21

Chapter 2 – What is Performance Punishment? 25

Chapter 3 – The Disadvantages of Being the "Go To" Person 30

Chapter 4 – When Perfectionism is Indeed the Enemy of the Good 36

Chapter 5 – When Working Harder or Smarter Isn't Necessarily Better ... 40

Chapter 6 – Recognizing What's the Symptom, and What's the Disease ... 45

Section 2 – An Out of this World Cure for Performance Punishment
.... **49**

Chapter 7 – Preparing to Launch: How To Use This Guide 51

Chapter 8 – Strategy # 1: Gain Control of Your Emotions 55

Chapter 9 – Strategy #2: Learn to Communicate Effectively 64

Chapter 10 – Strategy #3: Be Persuasive 70

Chapter 11 – Strategy #4: Establish Boundaries 79

Chapter 12 – Strategy #5: Document Your Situation
              Thoroughly and Be Brave 92

Chapter 13 – Strategy #6: Chart a New Course 98

Chapter 14 – Strategy #7: Above All Else, Remember,
              You're No Redshirt 107

Section 3 – What the Best Companies Do to Prevent
Performance Punishment **109**

Chapter 15 – Changing the Paradigm 111

Conclusion **119**

Chapter 16 – Putting It All Together 121

About the Author **123**

INTRODUCTION

Why Are We Here?

"Just when I thought I was out, they pull me back in."
Michael Corleone,
The Godfather: Part III (1990)

My journey to writing this book started in 2009. I was frustrated – no – miserable at work. I was working long, stressful hours to meet unrealistic deadlines only to receive more work with a dash of criticism on the side as the reward for my success. When I tried to lobby for an increase in compensation, I was reminded that I was lucky to have a job. I was running a highly productive team that I had built from scratch, despite the fact that my pay grade and title suggested that I was junior to my organizational peers with the same scope of responsibility. Together, my team and I were achieving business goals and making the executives we supported look good. My team was winning. My boss and internal clients were winning. Pretty much everyone I was working with, or for, was winning – except me.

I was caught up in the cycle of performance punishment and didn't even know it. Sound familiar? Then you've come to the right place!

Putting A Name On It

At the time, I didn't yet realize I had a boss who was trying to manage me out. She figured there was no harm in asking me to repeatedly do the impossible. If I was successful, it didn't matter to her because the job got done and she could regale management with stories of the team's success under her skillful leadership. If I was unsuccessful, it didn't matter to her because that was another arrow in her quiver to use against me when it came time for my performance review. If I tried to advocate for myself, she reframed it as complaining and added the conversation to her tally of strikes against me.

I was caught up in a no-win cycle of a very vicious kind. I knew I needed a change but couldn't see a clear pathway there.

When I vented to friends my about my situation, they somehow always found a way to help me find humor in it. In fact, we began to jokingly refer to the state I was in as "performance punishment" as a corollary to the truism we all knew too well: **too often, the reward for great work is more work.**

So I started talking to recruiters, career coaches and my mentors who all told me to do the same thing – start blogging as a means of building my personal brand and leverage my network to find a new opportunity.

As an undergrad, I was an English major. As a marketing and communications professional with over 20 years of experience and a Master's degree in Corporate Communications, writing had always been a part of my academic and professional life. So the suggestion made perfect sense to me.

It also scared me to pieces!

For some reason, the concept of writing publicly under my own by-line made me nervous to the point of inertia. When I was slow to take to the suggestion, my coaches explained, "Your job requires a lot of writing, so blogging is a great way to build your portfolio, demonstrate your versatility as a writer and develop your personal brand." The trouble was I knew nothing about blogging, how to promote or monetize my content, or do any of the things the best bloggers did to market themselves successfully. However, I took a leap of faith and started blogging anyway. Much to my surprise, my blog quickly came to serve two purposes for me.

First, blogging became my therapy – and in many ways, it still is. When something is on my mind, I tend to noodle it for a while, well, too long actually. My blog gave me a free space to hang my thoughts before they totally consumed me and prevented me from mentally moving on to the next thing. Through the process of blogging, I uncovered this truth about myself – I need a space to put my thoughts on paper, even if no one else besides me, and maybe my Mom, might ever read them.

Second, the process of trying to develop my blog took me outside my comfort zone in unexpected and positive ways. I had read somewhere that one way to drive traffic to your blog was to submit your posts to other sites for publishing. So I started to submit my posts about my parenting journey to parenting sites and my posts about my professional journey to career sites.

In doing so, I found that the advice I had received from my career coaches was spot on.

Conventional Career Coaching Worked, To A Point

My blog posts were actually getting re-published! I was SO excited to have found such a productive, therapeutic way to spend the 3+ hours a day I spent commuting. In addition, my blogging was helping me to create a meaningful digital footprint that recruiters were starting to notice.

In fact, I began to get contacted by recruiters in the un-posted job market, which I suddenly realized I was in due to the level I had reached in my career. Gone were the days that the jobs that paid what I was looking for could routinely be found via a newspaper or Internet ad, therefore, having recruiters come looking for me was increasingly necessary and something that the process of blogging helped me to achieve.

As relief from the challenges I was experiencing during my day job, I continued to follow the advice of my career coaches to the best of my abilities at that time. I hoped that if I couldn't find a way to do something different inside my company perhaps it would lead to a change on the outside. The problem was, I did so all without realizing that I wasn't focusing on solving my real problem.

I was doing the things that worked to help me get to the level where I was at, but had no clue how or what to do differently to get to the next level. Making matters worse, I was caught up in a cycle of performance punishment and didn't even know it.

Let me explain.

One Reorg Turned My Life Upside Down

A little over a year before I started blogging, I had been promoted into a management role. I was happily working above and beyond the call of duty to drive the changes the CEO I worked for at the time wanted in order to make her vision for the company a reality. I had the technical skills to get the job done, but I needed to develop softer skills like gravitas and mindfulness to become a more effective leader and influencer. While I could recognize these traits in others, I had no idea what they were called, let alone how to cultivate them in myself.

Fortunately, my boss at the time was extremely supportive of my efforts and rewarded me with praise, a salary increase, an outstanding performance review and the bonus that came with it. She also equipped me with the team that I wanted, a respectable budget, and the authority and air cover I needed to get things done. She also mentored and coached me about achieving and maintaining a balance between my work and personal lives. She encouraged me to work remotely on occasion and to invest in a gym membership and use it. She advised me to take unplugged vacations, trust my team and not to sweat the small stuff because "it all works itself out in the end."

During that year-and-a-half, I worked hard and achieved more than she (or I) ever expected. I turned the function I had been asked to lead around and felt invigorated by the challenge. The work we did was featured in our company's annual report and I was recognized with a trip to Germany to participate in a photoshoot and interview that landed me on the cover and made me the focus of a big spread inside.

I sometimes came in early and stayed late. I occasionally worked weekends and got much better about not checking emails while I was on vacation.

I was proud of my team, what we were able to accomplish and my ability to lead them.

I went home tired every night but satisfied that I had given it my all. Moreover, I was happy to get up and do it all again the next day.

Then it happened.

My Epic Battle with Performance Punishment

My CEO was promoted and made a member of our internal board of directors which meant I would report to someone else. A reorg or two later, I was reporting to someone who I later learned had gotten her job by questioning and criticizing everything my former boss, my team and I had built – without any context for the business objectives or environment in which it was all created. She was an expert salesperson, but my team specialized in marketing and communications. I soon felt no longer treated like I was valued for my expertise, track record, experience or contribution.

On a personal level, I had just been ordered by my doctor to complete 6 weeks of physical therapy which would have required me to work from home or out of our office a few miles away from my house (vs. the one that I commuted to which was an hour-and-a-half away) two days a week. Under the previous regime this would not have been a problem. But when, equipped with the doctor's orders in hand, I asked my new boss for a flexible work arrangement for 6 weeks, she flatly denied my request. When I tried to further explain my situation she replied, "I understand what you're saying, I just don't believe you." When I challenged that assertion, she qualified her statement, "I just don't believe you or anyone on the team should work remotely."

Adding insult to injury, shortly thereafter, she hired a new addition to our team who was based in another state and worked remotely from her home on a full-time basis. At least I was proposing to work out of our company's office in my same state! This would have enabled me to get treatment in the morning and still be productive the rest of the day since the commuter buses I normally relied on to get to New York City stopped running after rush hour.

She explained that what I viewed as hypocrisy was no such thing. She said that my new teammate was different because "We've worked together for many years at another company and I know her and can trust her to do what I want when I'm not around."

With no other obvious choice, I begrudgingly settled into my new professional life characterized by no work-life balance, constant criticism and mistrust. I came in early and worked late every day.

Ironically, while I increasingly felt like she was trying to manage me out of the company, she was constantly calling on me for help in areas that she was still learning more about. This introduced what I can only imagine was a heightened sense of insecurity on her part where I was concerned, which led the micro-management to turn into what felt like bullying. And as the criticism increased, so did my workload.

No Way Out

No problem, I thought. I have a good network inside the company and I'm part of a big global firm, so perhaps I can look for a job in another part of the company.

And that's when it happened.

Every time I had successfully interviewed with a different team internally, I was told, "We'd love to have you join our department but your manager will not approve the transfer. She says you're much too important to the work your team is doing right now and can't let you go for another six to 12 months and we cannot wait that long."

I was stuck – between the proverbial rock and a hard place. And, I had no idea what to do about it. It even made me begin to question myself as I looked for opportunities outside the company. This self-doubt showed up when I was interviewing for certain roles and it also prevented me from applying to others.

I hated going to work, but couldn't afford to just quit without having another job lined up. I was also afraid to take a day off for any reason given the perceived repercussions.

All the while, I couldn't understand why this woman I worked for, who I thought had such contempt for me, wouldn't simply let me go. Was this some unique form of sadistic management or corporate torture I hadn't seen before?

It wasn't until I began the therapeutic process of writing about my experience and the various strategies I was learning to use in order to get out of it that it occurred to me that I had, in fact, seen this movie before.

Literally.

On July 8, 2010 to be exact. That was the date LeBron James famously quit his first job as a professional basketball player in Cleveland through a televised ESPN special in which he announced he was switching teams to play in Miami.

When I thought about how the then talented forward had carried his team for seven years with the expectation that he would continue to do so for his entire career, something clicked. I realized it wasn't just me. It dawned on me **that if performance punishment could happen to rich and famous people like LeBron James, it could certainly happen to the likes of me**.

Watching him mature on and off the court over the next year also suggested to me that **breaking the cycle had more to do with the young basketball star evolving his thought process than it did with him changing teammates. To be happy AND successful, he had to change his mental processes and not just his employer!**

And Then Came WorkAwesome.com

In August of 2011, I would write a blog post inspired by my and LeBron's battle with performance punishment that was featured on WorkAwesome.com. While I hesitate to take credit for coining the term, the article is one of the earliest documented explanations of the phenomenon on the Internet.

In my WorkAwesome.com post, I asked and answered the rhetorical question, *Are You A Victim of Performance Punishment?*

Readers responded so passionately about the topic that I followed it with a piece that provided *An Out Of This World Cure for Performance Punishment* inspired by some of my favorite characters from *Star Trek*, the original series.

Together, those posts provide the foundation for the insights I will share in the first two parts of this book.

The last portion of the book draws from work I've done in my day job over the past ten years, focusing on what the best companies do to create and cultivate employee-friendly cultures that limit the potential for the phenomenon of performance punishment to thrive.

In between, I'll provide you with checklists, worksheets and other resources you can use to self-diagnose whether or not you're a victim of performance punishment and identify the steps you can take to deal with it. I'll also offer suggestions for people managers and employers to consider if they are looking to eliminate the phenomenon in their teams and organizations.

Like most books, mine is best read sequentially. But, if your situation is urgent, you can skip to the chapters that resonate most with your personal journey.

To put it simply, it doesn't matter where you start. Just…start! The longer you wait to make the changes needed to break your performance punishment cycle, the longer you'll wait to find your pathway to peace, happiness and fulfillment in your career.

When performance punishment goes unaddressed, it festers. As an individual, it can prevent you from opening yourself up to new opportunities. In organizations, it can deprive your team of your top performers and, worse, it has the potential to spread like wildfire.

The key is to identify performance punishment so you can take steps to contain it. The sooner you do so, the sooner you'll find your way back to a career situation that works for you as well as it does for your organization.

In the end, my hope for you is that you'll walk away with an assurance that you are not alone in experiencing this phenomenon and that you have the power within you to break the cycle. For the sports fans amongst us, my hope is that like LeBron James, you'll leave your performance punishment-oriented work situation and find your way back to one that makes you a champion!

I'll close this introduction by saying that my wish for you is simple: I wish you all the success you can handle and I hope is that in some way this book helps you to achieve it.

Take Away #1: You're not crazy and you're not alone. Performance punishment is real, but when it comes to breaking the cycle, identifying it is half the battle.

Why Am I Here?

Since this is the beginning of your journey in the fight against performance punishment, take a few moments to answer the following questions. We'll revisit them a bit later to check your progress.

Why did you decide to read this book?

```
┌──────────────────────────────────────────────┐
│                                              │
│                                              │
│                                              │
│                                              │
└──────────────────────────────────────────────┘
```

What three things do you hope to get from reading this book?

```
┌──────────────────────────────────────────────┐
│                                              │
│                                              │
│                                              │
│                                              │
└──────────────────────────────────────────────┘
```

If you feel that you are a victim of performance punishment, what aspects of your situation do you feel are beyond your control?

```
┌──────────────────────────────────────────────┐
│                                              │
│                                              │
│                                              │
│                                              │
└──────────────────────────────────────────────┘
```

What aspects of your situation do you feel you have the power to change?

```
┌──────────────────────────────────────────────┐
│                                              │
│                                              │
│                                              │
│                                              │
└──────────────────────────────────────────────┘
```

SECTION 1

HOW TO IDENTIFY PERFORMANCE PUNISHMENT

CHAPTER 1

Performance Punishment: The "King James" Version

"Jane, stop this crazy thing!"

George Jetson,
The Jetsons: Closing Credits (1962-63)

By all accounts, LeBron James is a great basketball player. Whether he plays for your favorite team or if you couldn't care less about the world of professional basketball, chances are you know his name. The 3-time NBA champion has been featured in a number of magazines, TV shows, movies and commercials. He's also responsible for one of the most controversial and epic job resignations in recent memory, all spurred on by what could arguably be viewed as his reaction to performance punishment.

An Akron, Ohio native, James was recruited to play for his hometown professional team, straight out of high school at the tender age of 18. His potential rags-to-riches-success meets favorite-son-turns-hometown-hero story captured the attention and imaginations of basketball fans around the world. He was the answer to Cleveland's struggle to compete. He was the hometown hero who would be the future, or perhaps even, savior of the franchise.

For seven years, LeBron did all he could to live up to the legend he was expected to be. From being named the league's Rookie of the Year to leading Cleveland to their first ever post-season appearance, it was hard to imagine the all-star player and 4-time league MVP doing more to help his team succeed. But his team wasn't winning. Despite a Herculean individual effort and one record-breaking performance after another, the goal of winning a championship repeatedly fell out of reach.

Fast forward to 2010 when James enters free-agency and is free to consider his employment options. The player now known as "King James" is quickly and famously courted by a number of other employers looking to recruit him to their team.

Many of us get a rush of excitement when we get a private message on LinkedIn from a headhunter looking to convince us to consider leaving our current employer for the one they represent. So, imagine this experience on steroids with teams offering you millions in salaries and bonuses while putting up billboards and developing other creative and expensive pitches to get you to switch companies. It sounds unbelievable but that's exactly what at least 6 teams did to convince the then 25-year old superstar to join their organizations.

And in the most epic, and perhaps, most infamous job resignation ever, James announced he was leaving his current employer in a TV special called *"The Decision."* He explained that despite how wonderfully his first employer had treated him, he felt it was time to go work somewhere he felt he could "be happy" and have "the best opportunity to win."

For seven years, Cleveland had given LeBron James the keys to the kingdom. And, night after night, his legendary performances became expected and viewed as normal with seemingly no promise of the ultimate compensation--a world championship--in sight.

I'm not a LeBron James fan per se, nor am I making any judgments about how he announced his famous decision, but I can only imagine that he might have been more than a little bit frustrated at the time.

Imagine if you were in his shoes. What if you were the sole go-to person on your team, carrying all the hopes and dreams of the company on your shoulders and your employer was slow to provide you with the human and other resources you needed to be successful? You too might jump at the chance to make a move in your industry's version of free agency.

In many ways, LeBron's first tour in Cleveland is a high profile but classic case of performance punishment. The better he performed, the more unrealistic the expectations of him became, until finally, the so-called rewards for his contribution began to include criticism from members of the media and fans who dared to call him overrated.

In other words, **James literally performed like a superstar until the rewards of doing so were no longer to his benefit.**

So while most of us will likely never quit our jobs via a televised special, if you've ever been a victim of performance punishment, you can begin to understand how **making a decision to move on in order to break the cycle is hardly ever just about the money.**

LeBron makes a good wage working for the team he's signed with, and likely, always will during his on-court career. When he left Cleveland in 2010, he had all the fame and fortune a kid with hoop dreams could imagine. He also realized that, like the rest of us, that's not what going to work every day is really about.

It's about finding what Miami represented to James at that point in his career. That is to say, **making a career is about working in an organization where the reward for great work isn't simply more work. It's about finding meaningful work, being happy and positioning yourself to do your best work on a day-to-day basis.**

For many of us, that process begins with recognizing that we're caught up in a cycle of performance punishment and then doing what we need to do to stop it.

Self Reflection:

Aside from my need to make money to pay my bills, what really motivates me to get up and go to work every day?

CHAPTER 2

What is Performance Punishment?

"Let's split up and look for clues."

Fred Jones,
"What's New, Scooby-Doo?:
Simple Plan and the Invisible Madman (#2.9)" (2004)

Simply put, **performance punishment is when you perform like a superstar and the so-called reward is to your detriment**.

Sometimes performance punishment is subtle – witness King James prior to his move to Florida. Many of us may find it hard to commiserate with a multi-millionaire who gets paid to play his favorite game for a living. But if you take a closer look at his situation at that point in his career, you might find that you have more in common with him than you think.

If it's a "LeBronish" case, **performance punishment is when your extraordinary performance on project after project becomes expected**. In turn, on the occasions when you perform at levels otherwise acceptable coming from your peers, you feel unfairly criticized. To further complicate matters, you take pride in always doing your best so your achievement orientation will not allow you to slack off and do less than your best. As a result, you feel caught in a cycle where more work and unrealistic expectations are your only rewards for your outstanding performance.

Performance punishment also occurs when are too valuable to the organization you're with in your current role for them to let you move on. So they prevent you from pursuing other growth opportunities, effectively putting what's good for the organization ahead of your goals and aspirations.

In their 2016 *Talent Mobility Study*, the Institute for Corporate Productivity (i4cp) refers to the managerial practice of holding on to top performers as "talent hoarding." They also report that "half of the 655 global companies and 74% of low performing organizations" admit to the practice which has a negative impact on company performance.

While the case of the NBA superstar isn't quite talent hoarding in the classical sense, the Olympian's employer knew he was valuable and never imagined he would ever think of wanting to move on – a mistake many employers and managers make in thinking about developing top performers.

Cleveland did everything they could to convince their hometown hero that theirs was the only game in town. And for years they succeeded. LeBron James knew in his head and his heart that Cleveland was where he should play. In fact, later in his career, he would return there to win his third championship.

However, when he first became a free agent, the fans in his home state never imagined he would ever leave, championship or no championship. By his own admission, neither did he. LeBron was a loyal, passionate and committed employee. As it turns out, they were both wrong. The money, the fame and the keys to the city weren't enough to make him stay. LeBron wanted more. Like many of us, he wanted an opportunity to grow and take his career to the next level. In his profession, the next level involves post-season play en route to a world championship.

In a more traditional corporate setting, top notch employers encourage talent mobility. They recognize that it's better to have a top performer move inside the organization rather than letting the talent walk out the door. According to research from the i4cp, "high-performance organizations are 4.5 times more likely to have the criterion for talent mobility transparent to their entire organization." The research firm also reports that high performing organizations invest in talent mobility, with "30% [saying] that talent mobility demonstrates to employees they have a future with the company."

Many organizations, however, sometimes miss the signs of performance punishment and those who don't, often handle it wrong.

The worst employers will say things like "Well, you're lucky to have a job." Or, "At least you have job security" if you bring your plight to their attention.

The better employers may ease your pain by throwing money at you or even creating a fancy title for you to sport . . . nearly anything to keep you their version of quiet and contently performing like the superstar they (and you) know you are in your current position. It's all good until you realize, they have you right where they want you—and they plan to keep you there as long as you're on the payroll!

And that's performance punishment in the best case scenario.

By now you're probably wondering, "But, being the "go to" person on the team isn't all bad, is it?"

Being the person everyone looks to in order to get the job done isn't a bad thing if you feel rewarded, fulfilled and otherwise appreciated for your efforts. In this case, you probably feel energized by conquering each challenge that being the "go to" person on your team presents.

If, however, you feel like your hard work isn't somehow worth the trouble, then performance punishment might be afoot. In a case of performance punishment, being the person everyone else can always count on offers more disadvantages than it does rewards. In the next chapter, we'll take a closer look at what this really means to see if you're dealing with a performance punishment scenario.

Check In: Is It Performance Punishment?

If it feels like this, probably not....	If It feels like this, probably so...
• I feel appreciated for my contribution. • I feel properly rewarded and compensated for my contribution. • I work hard and play hard. • I'm able to maintain a great balance between my professional and personal lives. • I don't mind coming in early or staying late every once in a while, it comes with the territory. • I feel like I'm continuously learning and have opportunities to grow in my current role. • I'm looking forward to my vacation, it will be great to unplug and relax. • I'm exhausted at the end of the day but feel good about all that I've accomplished.	• I was raised to work hard but it doesn't seem worth it. • Since I'm the top performer on my team, they're waiting to replace me before I can get promoted. • A stretch assignment they said I was perfect for opened up in another department, but my boss says I'm too valuable to the team and he can't afford to lose me right now. • I resent going to work because everyone else can go home on time but I'm always expected to stay late to get the job done. • When I told my boss I need additional support, she assured me I was talented enough to get by without it. • If I don't continue to go above and beyond it will damage my reputation and I can't deal with that.

The Performance Punishment Cycle

Step 1 – You pull off the impossible

Step 2 – You doing the impossible becomes expected as the norm

Step 3 – You feel frustrated and overwhelmed but are still compelled to
do an excellent job

Step 4 – You're asked to do the impossible, again

Step 5 – Go to Step 1

CHAPTER 3

The Disadvantages of Being the "Go-To" Person

"One of these days, Alice…"

Ralph Kramden,
The Honeymooners (CBS, 1955-1956)

Sometimes performance punishment can be disheartening and even mentally and physically taxing. In this case, the alleged reward for pulling yet another rabbit out of the proverbial hat is a heightened expectation about your future performance, leading to even more work without commensurate reward or compensation.

Let me give you an example.

You have a major, immovable deadline to meet at work, so you stay at the office an extra 4 hours before taking the project home to finish it. You sleep 3 hours, go into work early to polish the presentation and make your boss and your team look awesome to the higher ups.

Your boss and team toast your success later at the staff meeting with a chorus of "atta boys" or "atta girls" and you force a smile through a sigh, looking forward to some quiet time with your pillow as soon as it's quitting time.

The next week, your boss, faced with another fire drill, makes a beeline to your workstation even though you told him/her you have after work plans that night. In the months to come, you quickly realize you are now the "go-to" person on the team.

Your reward? More work. More responsibility. More stress. Longer hours. And fewer pats on the back because your proven ability to "save the day" is now your new normal.

In case you're wondering, that's performance punishment. But I digress. . .

So while you work late and get assigned all the missions impossible, your co-workers enjoy a nice balanced work life. They come in at 9:01 am after enjoying a leisurely cup of their morning coffee and then head off to take their kids (imaginary or real) to soccer practice promptly at 4:59 pm at the end of each day.

You, on the other hand, feel like you must come in early and stay late just to keep up with the mountain of work that keeps getting piled on your plate as the result of being one of the team's top performers.

Adding insult to injury, the one-time your co-worker has to work 30 minutes late, you find it impossible to empathize.

Good 'ol performance punishment is at it again!

Making matters worse, the one time you fail to successfully complete a mission that 007 and MacGyver together couldn't work their way out of, your boss wants to address it as a performance issue as he/she has "come to expect more of you."

And sadly, your boss is right. Your performance IS the issue. But not in a way you could have ever imagined!

That's performance punishment.

But is it just superstar athletes and overworked corporate types who are prone to performance punishment? No. **Performance punishment can happen in almost any kind of organization, in any sector and in any kind of role. It can even happen if you're volunteering or work in the public sector.** It is not a phenomenon that is unique to those of us with corporate backgrounds. In fact, as the case study at the end of this chapter shows, it can even happen in a sales organization where numbers typically rule all.

We'll talk later about how your company's culture plays a part in the cycle. However, more than that, there are a few characteristics that we all possess as individuals that may make us more susceptible to catching a case of performance punishment and affect our ability to break free.

Ironically, these traits are often the strengths that are the key to our success. The challenge is that we must learn how to keep our superpowers under control so they work for us and not against our ability to thrive in the workplace. For a better sense of who is prone to getting caught in a performance punishment cycle, read on.

Case In Point: Beware the Carrot at the End of the Stick

My husband is a great sales professional. Probably one of the best you could ever meet. He's also an excellent trainer, manager and leader who has an ability to bring out the best salespeople in others. So when he first joined the company he used to work for as a retail sales associate, it was no surprise that he quickly put up numbers that caught the attention of the company's senior management team.

Whether he worked in their lowest performing store or their top showroom, he consistently outperformed the other sales representatives, some of whom were store managers and others who had been with the company for many years. He quickly made his aspirations to move into management known and the leadership team was very receptive.

"Great," they said. "Let's give you a store to manage." "Oh yeah, we'll make your store our new training center so that new salespeople, store managers and general managers can learn how to replicate your success." In what seemed like no time, he went from being the top sales associate to being a top store manager and the trainer for the company's entire sales force, including the sales management team.

The problem was that because he had a unique indispensable talent that greatly improved the company's profitability, there was no clear-cut blueprint for how to fairly compensate him. They never really had an experienced sales trainer on the team before who could also sell and run a store all at the same time. So they did what most companies would do in that instance. They developed a compensation plan designed to make his talents work for the company at the best price possible. The result? Everyone else in the sales organization ended up making more money than he did.

The general managers he was training were senior to him and had a broader swath of responsibility, so their higher compensation relative to his wasn't a surprise. The other store managers who ran stores just like he did, and sent their people to be trained at his location, also earned more than him. The justification was that they had more experience running stores as he was promoted into the role. There was also a promise of bonus pay he would be eligible for since he was in a unique position to earn a bonus based on the performance of the people he trained. This opportunity to earn additional compensation, when introduced in a few months, would offer him earning potential other store managers didn't have. As a result, it seemed fair for management to pay him a lower salary relative to his organizational peers. "So, be patient," they said. "We'll take care of you."

A few months into his role as the company's first sales training manager, and after he had literally written the training guide for every role in the company's supply chain, management changed the performance bonus metrics for all salespeople. This change promised more money in theory, but in practice, set bonus targets that were nearly impossible to reach. Since hardly any of the sales people could qualify for the bonuses that he could share in as the one who helped them develop the skills they needed to be successful, he saw very little compensation for his widely-celebrated role as training manager.

In the end, most of the sales reps made more than he did too. Why? Because as a store manager he received a salary and company policy dictated that, in such a capacity, he was not entitled to earn full commissions for the sales he made. He was required to find a sales associate in his store to share them with.

Performance punishment had come to visit.

The pièce de résistance came a few years later when he was being considered for a role as a general manager. After doing everything his company asked him to do, including finding and grooming his replacement as store manager, developing and executing a highly effective sales training program, and turning their lowest performing stores into top performers time and time again, they promoted a new store manager that he had trained into the role.

Why? Because they couldn't afford to lose him as the sales trainer and because the numbers in his store were too good to risk a dip in revenue if they were to make a change in his store.

Performance punishment came for a visit and, in the process, found a permanent home in a sales-oriented organization where the numbers usually rule all.

CHAPTER 4

When Perfectionism is Indeed the Enemy of the Good

"I yam what I yam, and that's all what I yam."

Popeye,

Popeye The Sailorman (1933)

Performance punishment can be obvious or subtle. It can take place in any kind of organization and impact just about anybody. So, it's important that we know and understand ourselves so we can honestly assess our potential to be susceptible to it.

Anyone can fall victim to performance punishment, but perfectionists are among those most at-risk of finding themselves in such a scenario. Even if we don't consider ourselves to be perfectionists, most of us who are achievement-oriented will demonstrate perfectionistic tendencies from time to time. It's partly what makes us achievers to begin with.

Perfectionists, or those with perfectionistic tendencies, tend to fall victim to performance punishment because they push themselves and others to do their literal best, all the time. They also tend not to handle imperfections, let alone failures, of any kind very well. So, they strive to succeed at all costs and are harder on themselves than any manager could possibly be. Their bosses don't worry about whether or not they'll get the job done right, because they always do. They can't help it; they're wired that way.

If anything, they don't know when to let something go and have trouble accepting great work because only perfect work will do. While this can sometimes present challenges for the people who manage and work with them, it opens the door for performance punishment because their bosses and colleagues know they have great potential to step into that "go to person" position if the situation requires it. They know that the resident perfectionist is willing to come in early and stay late, or work through their vacation if need be, to get the job done. After all, it's what they do, whether their boss requires it or not!

For this reason, perfectionists with "go getter" attitudes are especially susceptible as they're the first to volunteer to take on assignments and will do whatever it takes to get the job done right.

But, **perfectionists aren't the only ones who can fall prey to performance punishment. Employees with these characteristics are also at-risk:**

- High achievers
- Self-directed
- Responsible
- Reliable
- Loyal
- Non-confrontational
- Conscientious
- Strong work ethic
- Problem solvers

The reason for this is simple. The same traits that make the people who possess them top performers are also the things help to get them caught of up in the performance punishment cycle.

In a performance punishment scenario, these strengths can manifest as weaknesses. That's what makes it such a difficult disease to diagnose and cure.

We are taught that all of these traits are key factors that contribute to success. And indeed they do. We cite them in job interviews and draw on them to fuel our feelings of confidence. In short, they are the secret weapons in our personalities that help to make us the "go to" players on our team.

As we saw earlier, being the "go to" person isn't always what it's cracked up to be, however. So while we should in fact cultivate our strengths, it's important that we don't let them keep us stuck in a performance punishment scenario. Similarly, our mental programming about working hard and being successful can also be a double-edged sword in the context of performance punishment.

We're often taught that the harder you work, the more you'll reap the rewards. Some of us are even taught to believe that hard work is its own reward. Conversely, we're not always taught that work life balance matters. Or that riches don't always come in the form of money. Or, if we are raised to believe in tenets like money can't buy happiness, it's all too easy to forget them when the bills are due, especially when you're being performance punished.

For many of us, it's not until we've had a wakeup call, often in the form of personal loss, health issues or worse, that we begin to put the importance of our work lives into healthier perspective. Add to that the stress of performance punishment and it's easy to see how you can feel like you're swimming in quicksand without a lifeline if you find yourself suddenly held back by your own success.

To put it simply, performance punishment at its worst, can create a view of your professional world where you feel trapped--where you don't trust yourself because going with what you know is what created the situation in the first place.

But in the words of my childhood hero Underdog, "There's no need to fear!" **You can break the cycle. But as in the treatment of all diseases, proper diagnosis is half the problem.**

I'll spend some time in the next section of this book discussing what you can do to break the performance punishment cycle.

But before I get to that, let me be clear about an important and difficult truth that must be dealt with in order to see the pathway forward more clearly. Working harder, or working smarter, is not the answer.

Vulnerability Check

What are my top strengths?	How could this strength make me susceptible to performance punishment?
Example: I have an eye for detail and take my time to ensure that things are done correctly.	*Example: I strive to succeed at all costs, which means sometimes, I may end up doing more than my fair share; my boss may also have unrealistic expectations for my performance relative to my peers*
1.	
2.	
3.	
4.	
5.	

CHAPTER 5

When Working Harder or Smarter Isn't Necessarily Better

"I was a victim of false doctrine."

Linus VanPelt,
Peanuts (November 3, 1959)

Working harder is not the cure for performance punishment. Neither is working smarter. Yet, if you suffer from the affliction, both are suggestions you may hear from family and friends who, with the best intentions, are trying to be supportive as you wrestle with this challenging phenomenon.

The truth is that in a performance punishment scenario, your work ethic is NEVER the problem in the sense that you need to work harder. Remember, working hard is partly what causes the vicious cycle you find yourself in to exist in the first place.

You, your boss, and everyone else who really matters already know that you work hard. In fact, that's partly how you became the "go to" person on your team, isn't it?

So, no, the cure for hard, thankless work is NOT more hard, thankless work.

Similarly, working smarter will not necessarily solve your performance punishment problem either. It sounds like a good idea, but your continuing quest to improve yourself and the processes you're responsible for is also part of the problem.

Consider that your ability to do things that previously couldn't be done, or to do them in ways that are better than ever before, is precisely why your boss believes you can handle more things to do.

There's a popular truism that says, "if you want something done ask a busy person." In my experience, busy people build their capacity to be productive by finding ways to improve their work processes so they can find the fastest pathways to efficiency.

In a performance punishment scenario, this becomes problematic because it enables you to take on more things to do. Since your superiors don't always have time to understand "how the sausage is made" so to speak, they just keep piling on the work. And the truth is, they don't have to care. From their perspective, it's why they pay you in the first place. Your reason for being on the team is to help them rest easy knowing that you'll take care of it…. again…. and again.

That is not to say you shouldn't work hard. You should. You should also strive to work smarter. However, in doing so, it's important to remember that the fundamental nature of performance punishment is to reward great work with more work. So working smarter or harder, will only result in, you guessed it, more work. As a result, neither of these holds the cure for your affliction.

The good news is that the cure for performance punishment is already within you – and with the tips and strategies discussed in section 2 of this book, I'll walk you through how to connect with these superpowers! However, there is one final precursor that is a critical foundational element to curing a case of performance punishment. That is, you must first be able to identify the symptoms apart from the disease.

Case In Point: No, You Standing There will Not Make the Copies Print Faster

In a previous work life, each quarter I was responsible for leading the process through which the CEO of the business I supported would prepare for his quarterly business update to the company's senior leadership, board and investors. This involved working with all of the senior executives who reported to him, in particular his CFO, to pull together a 100+ page PowerPoint presentation and supporting materials that would need to be printed, reviewed and edited several times in a series of prep sessions prior to finalization.

When I first got to the company, there was no support for this process. So our CFO and I would come in before 8 am and work past 8 pm for about 2 weeks in a row getting the iterations of the document printed out for each of the rehearsal meetings.

At first, the content and subject matter was completely foreign to me, so I had to come up a steep learning curve before I could begin to add strategic value to the content-side of our process. So, initially, I focused on figuring out how to improve the logistical side of the process, while I studied the ins and outs of the business.

The toughest part? Waiting for the aging color copiers on the floor to spit out the copies in time for each meeting. I'd send 7 to 10 copies of the monster document to the 3 printers on our floor, one of which was always guaranteed to be out of service at any given time.

Inevitably, papers would jam, ink would run out or my document would get stuck behind another one already in the queue. On more than one occasion, my boss would nervously stand over me as I tended to the machines, as if his being there would somehow speed the process along!

As time went on, I learned how to work smarter. I got to know the subject matter experts who pulled the materials together for the executives who contributed to the presentation, and I spent time learning about the business so I could proactively advise them on content. I also gained insight into their preparation process so that I could adjust our production schedule accordingly and build some cushion into our timelines. I found that by focusing on addressing our shared pain points, we quickly identified and implemented ways to make our collective lives easier.

Perhaps the biggest thing that helped me was that I made friends with a number of the seasoned executive assistants who supported the leaders who participated in the meeting. I offered them a greatly appreciated heads up on our quarterly process which I soon learned impacted their work lives as much as it did mine each quarter. In exchange, they happily provided me with much needed support in getting the copies of the deck proofed, printed and delivered on time. They knew which printers worked and where to go to make the administrative behind-the-scenes-magic happen and seemed proud to be part of what I affectionately began to refer to as my "dream team." By dividing and conquering, the materials were ready in a fraction of the time that it took when I was doing it all by myself.

I had successfully made my problem their problem since we all had a stake in seeing the executives we supported succeed (albeit in different ways). They felt empowered and a trusted part of a process that they too had grown frustrated with, but now had a chance to help make better.

My internal clients and superiors were so pleased with the efficiency I brought to the process, I received a top performance rating and was recommended for a promotion my first year.

But my promotion never came. Why? Because I had gotten so good at pulling off the yeoman's work that was the quarterly business review prep process, the challenging pathway it took to get there was soon forgotten.

I had streamlined the herculean effort that the project required so much that no one responsible for assessing my performance thought it was a big deal by my second year with the company. It had quickly become business as usual and expected as the new normal. Ironically, they actually gave me more kudos, credit and financial rewards when the process was broken, than after I had fixed it!

I remember calling all of the improvements I had made, along with the enhanced deliverables these changes had resulted in, to my boss's attention during my second annual performance review. I thought my performance in year two outshined the challenging inefficient process I overcame in year one by far.

He saw it slightly differently. "Yeah, but it was much tougher last year," he said. "Now, that process is much easier so you don't get credit for that anymore." I explained it was only easier because of all the work that I did and he half-jokingly replied, "So are you saying you're close to putting yourself out of a job because you don't have enough to do now?"

Performance punishment had struck once again.

CHAPTER 6

Recognizing What's the Symptom, and What's the Disease

"You can't handle the truth."

Col. Nathan R. Jessup,

A Few Good Men (1992)

The final and perhaps most difficult truth about performance punishment is that in order to free ourselves from its stranglehold on our happiness, we must face a very scary, yet empowering, fact – **it's up to us to stop it**.

Your evil supervisor really isn't the problem. Neither are your co-workers. They may be catalysts that add fuel to an uncomfortable fire, but in truth, they're more like a fever when you have the flu – they're a symptom and not the disease.

Remember the co-worker who was allowed to work remotely in my Introduction when I was not? She once confided to me that she too had the same challenges with our boss when they first started working together. Incredulous, I had to know what her secret was. After all, I thought, this new boss of mine was a horrible person who was literally ruining my work life. My co-worker then shared that her work life changed when she did something deceptively simple – she changed how she responded to our boss. At first the change in her behavior was met with surprise, but in the blink of an eye, a new normal was established between them. So while she had experienced everything I was going through, she broke the cycle by simply doing something different in the same situation. It was she who held the cure for her situation, not her boss.

To recap, your boss is only a symptom of your performance punishment problem. Chances are, so is your company's organizational culture. It's true that some company cultures are much more conducive to fostering performance punishment scenarios than others. It's also true that some organizational cultures limit the potential for it to thrive. However, having worked in both types of organizations, I can say my own propensity to get caught in a performance punishment scenario had more to do with my struggles than any organization did in and of itself.

In the most challenging cultures, whenever I suffered from performance punishment, I could see many of my co-workers thriving in ways that I was not. The difference between me and them wasn't skill set, experience or any of the conventional drivers of performance. It had more to do with the differences in how we navigated the professional environment that we shared.

As I matured in my career and became much more honest with myself, I began to learn and practice more and more of the techniques covered in the second section of this book. When I did, an amazing thing happened – I found myself building up an immunity of sorts to performance punishment scenarios.

In cases where I did feel a performance punishment spell coming on, I grew increasingly able to break the cycle much more quickly. I also got better at picking the organizations that were a better fit for me and that I felt would be truly supportive of my success. The truth that I came to realize was that my work environment, while important, mattered much less than how I responded to it.

Take Away #2: You can't always control a performance punishment situation, but you can always control how you respond to it.

How do you eat an elephant? One bite at a time.

Taming the beast that is Performance Punishment is the same as trying to eat an elephant. To do so, it helps to break down the components of the problem so you can solve them one at a time. Take a few moments to break your big problem down into smaller component parts. Of those, identify which aspects of your situation are beyond your control and make a conscious effort to not worry about them. Then, identify which aspects of your situation you either do control or can influence, then, focus your time and mental energy on solving those. You may be surprised to learn that you're more in control than you think!

What three to five aspects of your situation are most problematic?	Which aspects of your situation are beyond your control?	Which aspects of your situation can you potentially influence or change?
Example: I have no work-life balance.	*Example: Work hours. I can't work from home.*	*Example: My calendar – I can block out breaks during my day. I can usually control when I leave, especially if I check emails on my phone on my way home,*
1.		
2.		
3.		
4.		
5.		

SECTION 2

AN OUT OF THIS WORLD CURE FOR PERFORMANCE PUNISHMENT

CHAPTER 7

Preparing to Launch:
How To Use This Guide

"...if you've come this far, maybe you're willing to come a little further."

Andy Dufresne,

The Shawshank Redemption (1994)

B ack in 2011, when I first blogged about performance punishment, most who read my post could relate all too well. If you've made it this far, perhaps you can too. However, a few readers said my post was depressing as it hit a little too close to home for their liking. Perhaps you feel the same way having made it through the first section of my book. Or, perhaps you're encouraged knowing you are not crazy or alone in feeling how you feel as you work through this powerful phenomenon.

Either way, rest assured there is hope and a cure is possible.

Very early in my career I learned that if you were fast to point out a problem, you better come quickly with a solution. So instead of leaving readers with merely a description of the symptoms of performance punishment, I promised them and myself I would follow up with a prescription for the cure.

By now, you've probably gained some insight into my childhood and how I enjoy spending my free time consuming classic pop culture just by skimming the quotes at the beginning of each chapter.

It should come as no surprise then, in my search for a cure for performance punishment, I turned to some reliable sources for help – the advice of my own career mentors; books and articles I've read; workshops and training sessions I've attended; the comments of readers who responded to my post as it appeared on

WorkAwesome.com; and the always steadfast, insightful crew of the U.S.S. Starship Enterprise. Yes, I mean Captain James Tiberius Kirk, Dr. Leonard "Bones" McCoy and rest of the crew from *Star Trek* (the original TV series)!

Seriously.

A professor I had in graduate school convinced a class of over 100 students that we could learn something about management and leadership styles from the way the Enterprise was run and, well, let's just say the lesson spoke to me! While the content of that discussion is a book for a different day, I couldn't help but wonder…if Lt. Uhura and the boys could teach me something about leadership and team management, could they also teach me something about how to deal with performance punishment?

After some reflection on my own experiences and how I was able to break out of a performance punishment cycle at different points in my career, I identified seven strategies that can help to cure this particular affliction.

And if you're not a Trekkie or don't know *Star Trek* from *Star Wars* or a Star on the Hollywood Walk of Fame, don't worry. The characters are only starting points to the strategies covered, so no prior knowledge of *Star Trek* is required.

I've also included a number of tools and resources along the way to help you in your journey towards breaking the performance punishment cycle.

While there may be other tips and ideas you can think of to break the performance punishment cycle, these are the ones I've practiced most often in my professional life.

You don't have to use them all or even in order, with a few exceptions. Start with strategies #1 - #6 as they provide a foundation of skills every professional needs to either refresh or develop to boost their immunity to performance punishment. **The worst thing to do is to skip ahead to strategy #7 on charting a new course ahead before you've done the personal work needed to get ready for a new chapter.**

Remember, we are the sum total of our experiences and our experiences are a reflection of our decisions and behaviors. So, it's important to engage in some level of self-reflection and development before you change directions. If you don't, you risk winding up in the same situation but in a different work location.

And speaking of strategy #7, it's important to note that **charting a new course is not simply about finding a new job. So, if you're looking for a quick fix, that's not it**. The fix comes with doing the work needed to grow in the areas that you need to develop in order to change the paradigms governing your situation.

So feel free to use what many have called the "shopping cart" approach. Look at all the shelves and if you find something you need, put it in your cart, take it home and use it. If you don't need it, leave it on the shelf but know that it's there if you ever need to come back and pick it up later.

Lastly, you'll notice I've included a number of tools and resources along the way to help you in your journey towards breaking the performance punishment cycle.

So get ready. The process of curing your case of performance punishment begins in 3...2...1!

Tracking Your Ah-Ha Moments

As you go through this section of the book, use the first column below to capture any insights that you'd like to come back to as you work through your performance punishment scenario. Use the middle column to jot down action steps you can take to break the cycle. Capture any helpful resources, books, websites etc. that you'd like to revisit in your journey in the column to the far right.

Ah-ha Moment!	What can I do differently?	Resources

CHAPTER 8

Strategy #1 - Gain Control
of Your Emotions

"For what we are about to see next, we must enter quietly into the realm
of genius."

Dr. Frederick Frankenstein,
Young Frankenstein (1974)

Many times we get so stressed and emotionally worn out by performance punishment, that we can't be objective at evaluating what we can and can't control in order to change our situation. Often, the first step in curing this disease is to take time out in the form of a day or two off to remove ourselves from the situation so we can examine it and our options more clearly. The process of literally taking a step back introduces space between us and our circumstances and enables us to gain perspective on what's happening, as often, our emotions inhibit our ability to do so.

Of course this would be a very simple thing to do if we all had green Vulcan blood like Mr. Spock in our veins. But as humans, we must honor our emotions and find a positive way to deal with them so that our logical sides can balance our perspectives. So the lesson inspired by the U.S.S. Enterprise's first officer is simple: **take a time out to work through your emotions and logically assess your options—you'll likely find you have more than you realize!**

As an emotional being myself, I realize that this is MUCH easier said than done, especially in times of stress. So here are just a few ways that you can work on gaining appropriate control over your emotions so you can see things more objectively. The idea isn't to completely suppress the emotions that come with your humanity like Spock, but to corral your emotions so they don't skew your perspective about what's really happening in your performance punishment situation.

First, you must **learn to breathe**. Yes, breathe.

When I first started practicing yoga to release stress, I was surprised to find that every class started and ended with breathing exercise. I was even more surprised to learn that there were a number of different breathing techniques to use depending on my objective. For example, there are breathing techniques designed to help you clear your head of the challenges of the day. There are others to help you relax before a big presentation. And still other breathing techniques can help you get energized. The beauty of breathing exercises is that many of them can be done anytime and anywhere, with immediate impact.

My favorite breathing technique accompanies guided meditation, which I've come to learn is part of the practice of mindfulness. In a guided meditation, a coach leads you through the process of visualizing concepts, scenarios or situations, to help you literally see where you wish to be in your mind's eye. I know, it sounds a bit strange if you're not familiar with the practice. But you owe it to yourself not to knock it until you've tried it, as breathing and guided meditation are among the fastest pathways to achieving mindfulness.

Mindful.org defines mindfulness as "the basic human ability to be fully present, aware of where we are and what we're doing, and not overly reactive or overwhelmed by what's going on around us." As such, it can offer a great pathway to freeing yourself from the emotional burdens of your performance punishment situation.

Consider that during their wildly successful tenure with the Chicago Bulls, Phil Jackson and Michael Jordan both practiced mindfulness and credit it as a key contributor to the team's legendary "threepeat." Kobe Bryant has also cited his mindfulness practice as key to his success.

By finding a way to mentally slow things down and see things more clearly, and becoming more present in what was happening around them, these famous mindfulness practitioners gained greater control of the world around them. The good news is that you don't have to be an NBA champion to learn how to do this too.

There are a number of books, apps and websites that offer guided meditations and breathing exercises to help you begin and develop your mindfulness practice.

I started mine with some free apps that I would listen to during my 1.5 hour bus ride into New York City every morning. I found that spending my morning commute this way helped to center me and mentally prepared me for the day ahead. It also helped me to become more confident, strengthen my professional self-esteem, develop the gravitas I needed to act like a leader and calm my nerves in difficult situations. It also helped me learn to relax and get a better night's sleep.

When I first found myself in a performance punishment situation, I didn't know how to control my emotions, so my emotions controlled me. In doing so, they skewed my perspective and kept me in a cycle in which I could only see myself as a victim with no way out.

By developing a mindfulness practice, I learned how to honor my emotions, while gaining the clarity and confidence I needed to more accurately assess and respond to my situation. When logic played a bigger role than emotion in how I viewed my workplace challenges, the faster I was able to identify my options and chart a pathway towards pursuing my goals.

By now, you're likely having one of two reactions: "Yes, I'm going to start my mindfulness practice right now!" Or you may be a bit skeptical, thinking, "I'm not doing all that touchy feely stuff."

A few years ago, while dealing with the performance punishment scenario described earlier in this book, I attended a workshop on "emotional intelligence" offered through my job at the time. My initial reaction when I saw the topic on the agenda for the three-day training class was that this was more corporate buzzwords and mumbo jumbo. I thought it was going to be a waste of time, particularly since I was on deadline, so the training could not have come at a worse time.

To my surprise, the session turned out to be one of the most perspective-broadening experiences of my career. It tuned me into a tough reality about myself that was contributing to my performance punishment situation – I had a tendency to take things way too personally.

My husband is probably laughing if he's reading this, since he likely thinks I still do! And to some degree he's right. The difference is that now, I'm more aware of when I'm doing so and have strategies for making sure I don't allow things to get out of control when I do.

Making The Mindfulness-Emotional Intelligence Connection

In the class, they talked about self-awareness as a key to growing one's emotional intelligence or EQ. The workshop taught the principles outlined in *The EQ Difference; A Powerful Plan for Putting Emotional Intelligence to Work* by Adele B. Lynn. This included the author's 7-step process for developing your EQ of Observe, Interpret, Pause, Direct, Reflect, Celebrate, Repeat.

As I learned more about EQ, which Lynn defines as the process through which we learn "to manage ourselves and our relationships with others so that we truly live our intentions", I came to realize that when things went well, I took it personally.

By this I mean I reacted emotionally, often thinking that what I had accomplished somehow validated my position on the team or reflected my personal value at work. I was indispensable, so there's no way I could leave early once in a while or take time off. I had done the impossible, so of course I deserved my hard-earned seat at the table and would ultimately be recognized and rewarded for my efforts. I was happy with my performance but frustrated because I felt like doing my best was never enough.

The tricky thing was, that when things didn't go the way I wanted them to, I also took it personally. This meant that I reacted emotionally, often thinking how stressed out I was, unable to leave on time or take a day off and never able to get fairly compensated for my troubles. I was unhappy with my performance and frustrated because I felt like my best was not good enough.

By taking time to understand and learn how to develop my EQ, I came to face another difficult truth about my performance punishment situation – a good portion of the cycle I was experiencing was due to how I viewed my situation. There was no evil boss behind the curtain plotting against me. The corporate conspiracy to hold me back while others flourished off of my hard work didn't exist in the way that I had come to feel and experience it each day.

Yes, there was a lot of work to be done in a short period of time. Yes, I worked with a group of highly competitive people who would turn routine projects into a corporate edition of *The Hunger Games*. Yes, my boss expected a lot from me. But no, hindsight being 20-20, things were never nearly as bad as I thought they were at the time.

A big part of what was skewing my perspective was my own mental programming, which made me see things emotionally or take them personally. I thought I was simply passionate about my work and committed to doing a great job, no matter what. In fact, I was letting my emotions, including fear, rule my thinking. This made the otherwise challenging but manageable situation I was in seem much more insurmountable than it actually was.

People with high EQs have the ability to distinguish between their successes and failures and their own self-worth. They can separate the mechanics of a difficult situation from the feelings they may have about it. They can intellectually process difficult decisions and situations without attaching a self-defining emotional value to their circumstances or how they respond to them. They are also keenly aware of their own strengths and weaknesses. While they may get stressed when times get hard, they manage their stress, their stress doesn't manage them. They may have big jobs or responsibilities and somehow lead balanced lives.

In other words, they are able to do so, in part, by gaining better control of their emotions. That's precisely why so many of the world's leading companies invest in training courses like the one I attended designed to help employees learn how to develop their EQs. Some take this approach a step further by investing in resources like meditation rooms or on-site yoga classes that support mindfulness in the workplace. Why? Because neuroscience offers empirical proof that mindfulness techniques such as meditation actually have a positive, physiological impact on the brain.

But if you don't believe me, Google it. Or at least consider how the technology giant used these techniques to help its employees thanks to the efforts of Chade Meng-Tan, known as Meng.

Meng is a Google pioneer who helped to revolutionize the company's culture by developing a training program that connects the practice of mindfulness with the development of emotional intelligence, while demonstrating the scientific benefits of such an approach through neuroscience. The course he developed became the most popular of Google's internal training programs until the company established the *Search Inside Yourself Leadership Institute (SIYLI)* in 2012 as a separate, nonprofit organization to bring the training to the world's leading companies, nonprofits and government organizations.

It's important to note, that I've never worked at Google, nor have I attended any SIYLI programs so this is not a personal endorsement. I mention it here to simply make the point that some of the world's leading companies and brands have had great success by teaching their employees to practice mindfulness in order to develop their EQs. So imagine the positive difference you could make in your own professional life by doing the same.

According to social psychologist Dr. Ellen Langer, "The reason that work becomes dissatisfying is that people mindlessly assume that work has to be stressful. Stress is in the way we look at things, not in the experiences we actually have. People fall into a mindless routine and do things in the same way over and over again."

This is especially true and debilitating in a performance punishment situation. However, the good news is that **you can literally change your situation by learning to change the way that you think**.

Once your emotions are under control, you can see things more clearly. This sets the stage for effective communication – the next skill to master to conquer performance punishment.

Why Mindfulness At Work?

Benefits of practicing mindfulness at work include:

- Boost your emotional intelligence
- Boost your mental and physical health
- Reduce the impact of stress
- Improve your attention span
- Boost morale
- Increase your short-term memory
- Literally jog your brain
- Improve your focus
- Enhance your ability to handle criticism
- Improve listening skills
- Enhance interpersonal communication
- Prepare for leadership opportunities

Give Sama Vritti or "Equal Breathing" A Try

Many who practice yoga utilize this simple breathing technique to calm the nerves, get focused and manage stress.

1. Find a comfortable position.
2. Breathe in through your nose as you count to four.
3. Breathe out through your nose to a count of four.
4. Repeat.

You can close your eyes or not. If you like, increase the length of your inhalation and exhalation to six or eight counts as you become more comfortable with the technique. They key is to keep the length of the breath the same as you breathe in and out.

Recommended Reading

Mindfulness by Ellen J. Langer – In this groundbreaking work, the 'mother of mindfulness' explores the application of mindfulness in various aspects of life, including business.

The Mindful Athlete by George Mumford – Learn all about the practice of mindfulness directly from the man who taught it to Michael Jordan, Phil Jackson and Kobe Bryant.

Mindfulness on the Go by Jan Chozen Bays – It's said that Phil Jackson carried a copy of this wherever he went throughout his coaching career. If it worked for him, it could work for you!

Real Happiness At Work by Sharon Salzberg – Learn how to practice mindfulness in the workplace from one of world's top meditation teachers.

CHAPTER 9

Strategy #2: Learn to Communicate Effectively

"I may not be able to understand what you say when you say it, but before you say it, I can understand what you're going to say perfectly!"

Lucy Ricardo,
"I Love Lucy: The Ricardos Visit Cuba (#2.9)" (1956)

Aside from gracing the bridge of the Enterprise with her class and poise, Lt. Nyota Uhura served as the ship's Chief Communications Officer. With her signature Starfleet standard-issue ear piece and communications console she listened, filtered and analyzed all of the ship's messages—from distress signals to threats from the Klingons to undecipherable pulses to notices from Starfleet Command. Her job was to sort through all the clutter and escalate those messages requiring the Captain's attention. She also served as the conduit through which the crew of the Enterprise communicated with the rest of the universe.

As the ship's lead communications expert, she holds important clues for performance punishment sufferers. To understand how, you must first understand that communication takes place inside an organization on two levels: that is, there's "big C" and "little c" communications.

Communications with a capital "C" refers to departments inside companies and organizations that are formally responsible for how that organization communicates with various stakeholder groups, including the press, employees, investors, customers and other audiences. These departments often have names like Marketing Communications, Corporate Communications, Media Relations, Customer Relations or Investor Relations depending on the audiences they target. They serve as the brand's ambassadors for a given stakeholder group.

While not every organization has a function officially responsible for "big C", or formal Communications, every organization is filled with people who are responsible for "little c", or informal communications. These people are called employees. Yes, that includes you, even if you weren't an English or Communications major, hate public speaking and the thought of writing anything gives you hives. If you work for anyone, including yourself, you play an important role in how your company communicates with others. At a most basic level, you serve as a conduit through which others outside your organization come to learn about your company.

If you're a performance punishment sufferer, working to fine-tune your "little c", or informal communications skills should be an important part of your prescription for stopping the cycle. Why?

Performance punishment thrives in environments where communication breaks down. The trick to breaking the cycle is to break the silence and find a means of communicating clearly and confidently with your colleagues and manager. You must learn to clarify and articulate your position, along with what you need from them in order to be successful.

The worst thing you can do is crawl into your shell and suffer silently. This is not to say that complaining to any and everyone who will listen to your plight is the answer. However, as we saw earlier, finding a way to engage others in your problem solving is often critical to the solution-finding process.

In practical terms, it's the difference between how one of the world's most famous cartoon dogs and some meddling kids attempt to solve the mystery at the beginning of every episode in the *Scooby Doo* franchise and the end. When the ghost ship with the phantom pirates first shows up at the beginning of the episode, the gang always splits up and searches for clues. While splitting up sets the stage for some comic relief and some accidental clue-finding along the way, the gang really doesn't accomplish too much that's purposefully productive in the process.

Everything seems to change by the end of the episode, however, when the gang joins forces to look at all the clues together and come up with a plan to catch that villain. And while, as in real life, things don't always go 100% according to their plan to trap the ghost, together they always manage to save the day. The moral of their story is don't split up. You stand a much better chance of catching the ghouls and solving the mystery by working together.

The same is true in your fight against performance punishment. **By enlisting the guidance of a confidant, mentor, colleague or friend, you can begin to strategize ways to approach your situation differently.** Work with them to deal with your emotions first. If you need to lean on them for a therapeutic scream or cry, do it. But remember, only pep talks and actionable advice are allowed—no pity parties! As Patti LaBelle so wonderfully says in *Love Never Dies*, you need to "Fluff up, baby. Beat your face into place. Get back in the race" as soon as possible.

So before the pity party has a chance to begin, turn your focus to brainstorming ideas for addressing the problem. Have your gang help you to think through the answers to key questions such as...

- In this situation, what am I doing well?
- Are there any skills or competencies I need to develop to be successful?
- How does the process I'm challenged with work?
- How can the process be improved? What resources or support do I need to do so?
- What's really important to my boss? Am I delivering that already?
- Is there an opportunity to make my problem someone else's?
- What is my goal? How does my organization define success? Where are the connection points between the two?
- What does my boss really need and want from me?
- What do I really need and want from my boss? What are the opportunities to bridge the gap?
- If I could help my boss understand one thing about my situation, what would it be?

Use these prompts as a starting point to think through your situation more clearly.

Then, **begin to plan the conversation that you need to have with your manager or whoever is in the best position to help you break your performance management cycle**. In this part of the communications planning process, think about how exactly you wish to structure your conversation:

- What is my objective? What do I want to achieve as a result of this conversation?
- What specifically am I asking for? What questions or considerations might my boss have?
- What exactly am I trying to say? If my boss hears nothing else, what do I want him/her to take away?
- What agreements did we reach? What steps should I take next? By when?

By taking the time to turn your thoughts into a more structured conversation, you greatly improve your chances of being heard.

Knowing your audience is key to your preparation. As you prepare, keep your eyes and ears open for clues about how best to communicate your position more effectively.

- Does your boss prefer face-to-face meetings, video conferences or email?
- Is your boss driven more by numbers or qualitative assessments?
- Do they respect or resent pushback?

Once you clarify your point of view and understand how others want and need to hear from you, you'll be better positioned to prevent performance punishment from creeping up on you and taking over.

When your agenda for the discussion is ready, arrange the meeting. Share your objectives for the discussion early to make sure your expectations are aligned. During the conversation, focus on listening more to *WHAT* your boss is saying, than *HOW* it's being said.

Before you leave the discussion, make sure you clarify next steps. Is any follow up required? Can you schedule another check in for a month from now? Will you be sending through any additional documentation? The best salespeople know how to "ask for the order" and close the deal. You have nothing to lose except for the case of performance punishment you're currently dealing with, so don't be afraid to ask for what you want.

Even if you don't get everything you're asking for two things will happen. First, you'll feel like a weight has been lifted off your shoulders since you've finally made your position known. Second, the stage for at least incremental progress will have been set. No matter how you look at it, progress, however small, will have been made. So go for it! The only thing you have to lose is your case of performance punishment.

If things don't go perfectly in your first conversation, try not to worry. In fact, closing your conversation with a recap of what you discussed, including any agreements and next steps is a great way to close the conversation and set the stage for the next one. If all else fails, simply close the conversation with one simple question: "Thank you for your time today, it was really helpful. Can we sit down again in 1 to 2 weeks so I can update you and help to keep the lines of communication open?" You can tailor your phrasing for this question based on your situation, but the idea is to ask for the opportunity to sit down again in a reasonable timeframe so you can keep the one-on-one conversation going.

Effective communication takes planning and practice. The more you do it, the better you'll get at it. In the next chapter, we'll take a look a few time-tested techniques you can use to enhance your communication skills by tapping into your passion, credibility and logic so you can become more persuasive.

Communications Do's and Don'ts

DO ask for what you want – remember if you don't ask, you will never get.	**DON'T let fear or emotion rule** the conversation
DO ask questions. Managers and senior leaders LOVE to ask questions as most of them tend to be intellectually curious. As leaders, they also appreciate it their team members seek guidance. So speak to them in a language that they'll understand.	**DON'T complain.** No one wants to hear it and it will not get you want you want.
DO get to the point. Managers tend to be very busy people to make the most of your time with them.	**DON'T discuss other people,** focus on the process instead.
DO help them see what's in it for them.	**DON'T throw other colleagues under the bus** in your discussion. That tactic reflects poorly on you and it only take one organizational restructuring before that can come back to haunt you.

Guide to Structuring Your Conversations

"The Ask" What do I want to achieve?	Questions to Consider What do I want my boss to think about? What am I unclear about?	Key Messages What Point(s) Do I Want to Convey?	Agreements What Happens Next?

CHAPTER 10

Strategy #3: Be Persuasive

"There is no fire, Fred. There's nothing to burn in Bedrock, everything is made of stone."

Barney Rubble,
"The Flintstones: Arthur Quarry's Dance Class (#1:16)" (1961)

If you've ever fallen victim to performance punishment, chances are you are passionate about your work and have a high degree of knowledge or skill in a particular area. Around the office, you may even have a reputation as a "miracle worker" and when asked to do the impossible, your default setting may even be to initially push back. Pushing back initially can be an effective tactic to employ in order to buy yourself more time to figure out how to accomplish the task at hand. If you're not proficient in how to push back, don't worry, I've got you covered with strategies on how to develop this skill later on in this book.

But, perhaps you've got a co-worker who is knowledgeable, occasionally emotive, and known to passionately advocate his or her point of view when things get a little hectic around the office. In other words, perhaps you work with someone like the Enterprise ship's Chief Engineer Montgomery Scott.

Scotty was extremely passionate about his work and his ship. He gained a reputation as a "miracle worker" because he literally knew the Enterprise better than anyone. When asked to do the impossible, his default setting was often to initially push back. This was a tactic he successfully employed to buy himself more time to figure out how to recharge the dilithium crystals or to fix the proton torpedoes. He was also known to passionately advocate his point of view in times of crisis by saying something like, "She's going to blow!" or "I'm giving her all she's got, Captain!"

The thing about his outbursts was that, while emotionally charged, they never became personal or took Scotty's focus off addressing the issue at hand. He expressed his point of view, put the facts on the table for the Captain to consider, highlighted his concerns and managed expectations without holding his tongue. But all the while, he never allowed his professionalism or his judgment to be ruled by his passion.

In dealing with his emotions, Lt. Scott found a way to express himself and keep the main thing the main thing. He was great at passionately advocating his position and explaining the technical pros and cons of a situation to his management so that a solution that served the greater good could ultimately be found. In doing so, **Scotty was truly a master of the art of persuasion. When attempting to break the performance punishment cycle, you must learn to do the same**.

As noted earlier, a key step in breaking the performance punishment cycle is to gain control of your emotions in order to enable your audience to hear what you're saying. Admittedly, since most of us don't have Mr. Spock's mixed Human and Vulcan heritage, controlling your emotions when you're being performance punished is a very difficult thing to learn how to do. However, if Scotty could find a way to persuade others by effectively dealing with his emotions at work and letting his technical expertise and experience be his guide, you can too.

So no, I'm not suggesting that you act like Scotty and shout "The copier's going to jam up, Frank! We'll never make it to the meeting in time!" the next time your boss wants you to send 20 copies of that 75-page power point presentation to the copier 2 minutes before you plan to present it.

The key is to learn how to advocate for yourself and your solution with passion. Trust in your technical skills, knowledge and experience and let them lead you as you manage expectations and make your case. In short, look to find ways to use your passion as you look to persuade others to consider your position. Remember, **being persuasive is as much about being credible and reasonable as it is about being passionate**. Scotty knew this and used his impassioned pleas to buy himself the time he needed to save the Enterprise in many an episode.

But you don't have to take my – or Scotty's – word for it. In his legendary treatise, *Rhetoric*, Aristotle artfully articulates how the forces of credibility, reason and passion help speakers to make effective persuasive arguments.

If you've ever taken a public speaking class, chances are you've studied the principles of Aristotle in the section of the course focused on persuasive presentations. In case you're not familiar with the ancient Greek philosopher's views on rhetorical theory, here's an overly simplified recap.

Aristotle identified three methods of persuasion that speakers should use to make their point – ethos, pathos and logos. Ethos relies on the credibility of the speaker. Pathos is the process through which the speaker appeals to the emotions of the audience. Logos involves convincing the audience through logic and reasoning. The most powerful speakers, litigators, teachers, entertainers, artists, coaches, politicians and communicators use all three.

If you're a victim of performance punishment who is looking to persuade others to see or do things differently, one or more of these approaches can also be effective. The key is to use the tools of Aristotle to frame your argument in manner that is indeed persuasive instead of making your case in a manner that might be perceived as complaining or negative.

For example, in your performance review conversation with your supervisor, **you can use ethos to establish your credibility in spaces that fall outside your job description**. This might include describing the many unofficial hats you may wear in a given process or project, or calling attention to awards and recognition that you've received.

An executive assistant, for instance, might also be the lead event planner for a quarterly meeting or a junior team member might regularly demonstrate team-building skills typically expected by more senior roles in the company. Or, you may want to convey how you've completed a rigorous training program or achieved an industry designation to underscore how you've gone the extra mile.

Instead of…	Try ethos-oriented statements to demonstrate your credibility and role in the company's success.
"I'm tired of not being recognized as the top sales person."	"In the past 6 months, I've gone from the bottom to the top of the leaderboard, earning my way into the inner circle of the President's club and the company's designation as a platinum-level producer."
"Every quarter I go above and beyond to get the project done and you never seem to notice."	"My greatest strengths are my collaborative style and ability to work with colleagues at all levels of the organization. The ability to work with, learn from and lead the virtual team I've assembled to get the job done in the face of aggressive deadlines and limited resources."
"In addition to being your best customer service rep, you continue to dump extra work and special projects in my lap."	"I successfully completed Sales and Service Ninja training and my customer satisfaction scores earned me the Hero Award from our outside research firm."
"You and I both know that the canned food drive was much more successful with me leading it."	"Here's a copy of the certificate of accommodation and a letter I received from the food bank thanking me and the company on this year's record-breaking effort."

You can **draw on pathos to communicate your dedication for the work and passion for a project**. You can express how you'd love to get more training or partner with others in your process to enlist more help. You can articulate that you're proud of the results that the team has achieved under your leadership. You can also express how much you enjoy working on the team but need your manager's help and support in order to strike a more effective work-life balance to maintain your current level of performance.

Instead of...	Try pathos-oriented statements that allow your passion to come though while showcasing your contribution.
"I'm tired of not being recognized as the top sales person."	"In addition to all that the numbers demonstrate I've accomplished as the company's top salesperson this year, I've proudly served as a company spokesperson, representing the firm at our industry's leading recruitment and training events. In addition to helping to attract top talent to the firm, these additional responsibilities have enabled me to share my passion for the company and its products with others."
"Every quarter I go above and beyond to get the project done and you never seem to notice."	"One of the things that first attracted me to this role was the chance to work with smart people to make a positive difference. The chance to change things for the better and leave my mark on the world is what gets me up in the morning. So, while our quarterly production process is challenging and requires tremendous effort, I'm proud of the leadership role I've played in helping to make our quarterly process more successful."
"In addition to being your best customer service rep, you continue to dump extra work and special projects in my lap."	"I really enjoy problem solving and interacting with people, which is why I've been so successful in my customer service role. At the same time, I enjoy the various special projects I've had the opportunity to lead. I would love to discuss how to balance those so I can bring the best of my problem-solving and interpersonal skills to both situations even more effectively."

"You and I both know that the canned food drive was much more successful with me leading it."	"I have a true passion for giving back to my community. I'm involved in a number of charitable causes and community service projects outside of work, so when the company needed a new leader for the food drive this year I jumped at the chance to bring my personal and professional passions together. I'm very proud that we were able to collect more food this year than ever before and that through my leadership we were able to inspire more employees to give and ultimately help to enhance the lives of more people in the process."

Finally, you may **use logos to present your manager with facts that support your point of view that you're making a contribution that is above and beyond the call of duty.** This can come in the form of business results that you've generated, testimonials from colleagues that have witnessed you in action or other metrics you can think of to measure your contribution and success.

Instead of...	Try logos-oriented statements to present facts that empirically prove your success.
"I'm tired of not being recognized as the top sales person."	"Over the past 6 months, I've been the company's top producer. I've grown sales by 35% compared to a 12% growth rate garnered by the rest of the team."
"Every quarter I go above and beyond to get the project done and you never seem to notice."	"The new process I introduced has cut production time by 8 business days or 75%. It's also saved us $10,000 in production costs, reducing our overhead by 15%."
"In addition to being your best customer service rep, you continue to dump extra work and special projects in my lap."	"Since the beginning of the year, I've completed 8 special projects and have earned a customer satisfaction rating for my service of 98%."

"You and I both know that the canned food drive was much more successful with me leading it."	"Under my leadership, the office collected 3,578 cans of food and raised $7,598 to support our local food bank. This is an increase of 1,558 cans of food and $3,585 over last year."

Each of the sample statements provided offers compelling evidence in support of the speaker's superior performance and reframes the performance punishment-oriented sentiments into the basis for a much more productive conversation. Taken separately in each of the four scenarios presented, they are effective in using the tools of Aristotle in their own way. Taken together, you can quickly begin to see how powerful they can become in helping the speaker break free of the emotional stranglehold of performance punishment to put forth an argument that stands a better chance of being heard.

Understanding the Ethos, Pathos, Logos Connection

Sample Speech	Method of Persuasion	Why It Works
"Ladies and gentleman, the President of the United States..."	Ethos	The audience immediately gives the speaker credit for being a knowledgeable authority simply by virtue of their position.
"Throw your hands in the air and wave them like you just don't care..."	Pathos	Creates excitement to drive listener engagement and enables the speaker to make an emotional connection with the audience.
"4 out of 5 patients were cured..."	Logos	Uses facts to make the case.

Inspired Communications

Think of a time when your mind was changed by a speaker, communication or performance and jot it down in the first column below. Use the adjacent columns to identify how Ethos, Pathos and Logos played a part in how you experienced the message.

Communication that changed your mind	Use of Ethos	Use of Pathos	Use of Logos

Advancing Your Perspective

In thinking of your own performance punishment situation, use the worksheet below to think about your point of view. What do you want others to understand or change relative to your situation? Then, think about Aristotle's toolkit and think about the kinds of arguments you can make to advance your perspective:

- Should you try to build your credibility or establish your authority? (Ethos)
- How can you get your audience to make an emotional connection to what you're saying? (Pathos)
- Or, would a fact-based approach be more effective? (Logos)

Then, try to craft a few sample statements that you utilize as talking points when you have the opportunity to make your case. Feel free to use more than one method of persuasion. Remember, the most effective orators find a way to incorporate all three methods into their communications.

Your Point of View	Method(s) of Persuasion	Sample Statements

CHAPTER 11

Strategy #4: Learn to Establish Boundaries

"I've written a new and improved roommate agreement which benefits me greatly. I'd like you to sign it."
Dr. Sheldon Cooper,
"The Big Bang Theory: The Agreement Dissection (#4.21)" (2011)

Part and parcel to curing any case of performance punishment is learning how to set healthy boundaries with your boss, your colleagues and yourself.

In *Star Trek*, Dr. Leonard "Bones" McCoy was the Enterprise's chief physician. He was also one of the Captain's "go to" guys — a role the cantankerous doctor didn't always enjoy. To let the Captain know where he stood on the issue of the day, Bones uttered his famous catch phrase on more than one occasion: "Dammit Jim, I'm a doctor not a {insert role beyond his skill set he was asked to play here}!"

For clarity, I'm not suggesting that you quote Dr. McCoy verbatim the next time an urgent situation stresses you at work. Turning to your boss and saying, "Dammit Linda, I'm a software engineer not a magician!" the next time the copier jams, might earn you a one-way ticket to HR.

However, learning to establish firm boundaries when someone tries to push you to do the impossible, again, is a key step in breaking the performance punishment cycle. So, the lesson from Dr. McCoy is a simple, yet important one: **Know your limits and know when (and how) to say No!** Here are a few strategies to help you learn to do just that.

Take a consultative approach to managing expectations – The process of learning to manage expectations is important because it sets the rules of engagement in any relationship. By learning to treat your boss or colleagues like clients in a consulting relationship, you can set certain boundaries in your relationships up front, and stop the performance punishment cycle in the process. If you need a little extra help in this area, at the end if this chapter, I've included 5 principles you can follow to do this based on my years of experience in various consulting roles.

Make a date to take yourself to lunch – While all of us will find the need to desk dine from time to time, if you're caught in a cycle of performance punishment, you must find the discipline to lunch away from your desk, regularly. This sends a message to others that for at least a few minutes each day, you're unavailable. Remember, the CEO and the President of the United States both take lunch once in a while, so you can too. In addition to giving yourself a much needed change of pace and scenery, taking lunch away from your desk gives you a chance to interact with coworkers or colleagues, including those in your network from other companies. Besides, you're entitled to the mid-day break so take it.

When I first learned to do this, I would block out 30 or 60 minutes on my calendar every day so that other meetings couldn't creep into my lunch time. Then, I practiced being away from my desk when that time was scheduled.

By treating my midday break like a meeting, it reset others' expectations around my availability for a short period during the day and enabled me to give myself an opportunity to take the break I was entitled to.

In time, I felt much better about popping into my boss' office during times when we were especially busy to say, "I'm going to grab a sandwich, but I'll be back in an hour. I have my phone with me, so if something urgent comes up while I'm gone, send me a text and I'll be right back." To my surprise, my boss never called me back from lunch early, even when I thought things might fall apart in my absence. In time, my boss also stopped looking for me at lunchtime. This part of my performance punishment cycle had been broken!

Leave no vacation day behind – Use your vacation days. Don't lose them. I know you might feel like you have too many things going on at work in order to take a day off, but consider that the CEO and even the President of the United States both take time off to regroup and recharge. So why can't you? Chances are, the thing that's really preventing you from taking some much-needed time off is your perception, which, as we've seen, can be skewed if you're in a performance punishment situation.

In the mid-1990s, I worked for a leading Wall Street brokerage house. I had a co-worker who had been with the company for many years. He was well-liked and well respected, partly for being a great person and partly for his dedication to the company. He had a family but often worked late and on weekends.

One Monday morning, I was called into my boss' office to write a letter to the company informing them that this beloved colleague had literally died at his desk sometime between when the rest of us left for the weekend on Friday and when the weekend cleaning crew came in and found him on Saturday. He had died of a heart attack, likely brought on by stress those closest to him openly speculated.

The crazy thing wasn't being asked to write such a sensitive communication at a relatively early point in my career. To me, the crazy thing that about the situation that has stuck with me over the years was that by the time I had gotten to work on Monday, his desk had been largely packed up, his computer reconfigured and workstation made ready for whoever the next occupant would be. For all his dedication, and for all the kind words we ultimately wrote about him and how he'd be deeply missed for his contributions, the company had already moved on. And, it hadn't even been a full business day later. I realized then, **that there is no such thing as an indispensable employee in the workplace**.

The moral of this particular story is to **always remember that you're working to live, not living to work**. Your mind and your body need time to rest and recharge. And, yes, there are worse things than a poor performance review, losing your job or whatever you're afraid of that's keeping you from taking some time off.

For several years *Harvard Business Review* and the U.S. Travel Association have studied the connection between employee well-being and vacation time. Their *2016 Project: Time Off* study found that most (55%) American workers do not use all their vacation time.

The study also asked why people left so much paid vacation time on the table. Feelings of being indispensable, or that it was impossible to do so as they advanced in their career, or the need to demonstrate dedication all topped the list. Sound familiar?

Consider that the study also found that employees who took 11 or more vacation days were 30% more likely to receive a raise and those who took more than 10 days off were 65.4% more likely to receive a raise or bonus.

The study also shows that to benefit from vacation time, you must use the time to disconnect, regroup, rest and recharge. Simply taking time off and checking emails, taking calls and working your way through it completely diminishes your ability to be productive when you officially return to the office.

So plan your stress-free vacation carefully. You deserve it. The company will go on without you…and so will you! Your family, productivity and your mental and physical well-being will all thank you for it.

Strategically drop the ball if you need to – The next time you're about to hyperventilate because you're not getting the job done in record time, pause. Then ask yourself "what if this didn't get done right this second?" The answer might surprise you. You might realize that the task you're obsessing over and the thing that is making your stomach churn can…actually…gasp…wait.

I'm not saying to trade in your overachiever ways to become a slacker. No.

What I AM saying is that sometimes when we're in the moment, and we're in crunch or "get it done" mode, the things that we're focused on and are causing us stress aren't really the grand emergencies we view them to be. Sometimes, the task at hand really CAN wait until tomorrow. For us overachieving perfectionists, with work ethics of steel, this can be a very hard thing to wrap our heads around. So taking a moment to pause to regain your perspective is important.

Ask yourself, "What would YOU do?" – Try imagining it's not you in your situation, but your best friend, your child or someone else whose success you truly care about. Wouldn't you tell them, "It's well past 8 p.m. and you've been there 12 hours already. Come home. Whatever you're doing isn't that important."

Of course there are professions and situations that require long hours, late nights, early mornings and even some occasional mind-reading and firefighting. However, performance punishment makes EVERY job and EVERY task feel that way, all the time. The key is to retrain your brain to recognize the difference.

Remember how to eat the elephant – As mentioned, there's an old adage that asks and answers a key philosophical question in life. The question: "How do you eat an elephant?" The answer: "One bite at a time."

The idea is that in order to complete an insurmountable task that is the proverbial elephant in the room that you're trying to deal with, the key is not to try to eat the whole thing at once. To be successful, break down your challenge into smaller bites that are easier to digest.

When it comes to resolving your performance punishment-induced workload, you must do the same. Avoid the inclination to tackle the whole project at once. Instead, break down what must be done into smaller parts. Then, tackle those parts one at a time.

Doing so provides a great way for you to set a mental boundary in the sense that it stops you from pressuring yourself into doing too much at once. It also gives you a pathway back to an otherwise elusive sense of accomplishment as you complete each smaller task on your list.

The next time you're overwhelmed and don't see an end in sight, ask yourself the following questions to figure out how to eat the elephant in the room:

- What are the tasks that make up this project?

- Which tasks can I do quickly? Which tasks will take more time?
- If I can only complete one task in the next hour, what should it be?
- What items on my "to do" list can wait until tomorrow?
- If I were advising my best friend how to handle this situation, what advice would I give them?
- If I don't get this done right now, what will happen?

You can use the worksheet at the end of the first section of this book to map out your plan for breaking your big challenge down into a series of pieces that are a bit more digestible.

Learn to advocate for yourself – The concept of self-advocacy grew from the movement to win civil rights for people with disabilities. In the simplest of terms, it's about empowering disabled individuals to speak up for and take care of themselves. Educators and academics have evolved the conversation around self-advocacy to encourage students of all abilities to understand their needs and ask for the support necessary to address them.

Autism Speaks offers this definition of self-advocacy on its website:

"Self-Advocacy is:

- speaking up for yourself,
- asking for what you need,
- negotiating for yourself (working with others to reach an agreement that will meet your needs),
- knowing your rights and responsibilities,
- using the resources that are available to you,
- being able to explain your disability either by the use of written words, pictures or gesture."

As a parent, these concepts and principles resonate with me deeply as my husband and I have worked to teach our kids to practice them. As a professional who has dealt with a case or two of performance punishment at various points in her career, they do as well. They provide an excellent framework for self-reflection and identifying opportunities to break out of a performance punishment cycle.

Use the worksheet at the end of this chapter to take a moment to think about each of the self-advocacy principles and brainstorm a strategy or two for each that you can put into practice to break free of your performance punishment situation. In addition to helping you to develop your personal action plan for finding a cure, the practice of writing down your thoughts, as you'll see in the next chapter, is a powerful tool in the process.

5 Principles for Managing Expectations More Effectively

There are many strategies for managing expectations more effectively. Here are five that I've often relied on in my 20 plus years working in a consulting or advisory capacity to a broad range of internal and external clients:

1. **Set the tone up front** – Hold an introductory or initial project kick off meeting. Remember, your job is to guide your client in the discussion so they will understand how you work; which aspects of the work you can or cannot handle in house or with existing resources; when you are (or aren't) available; how their project will move forward if you're out of the office; what you need from them in order to successfully complete their project on time; what they can expect during each phase of the project; and what deliverables will be due and by when.

Tips for success:

- Understand your own workflow or process, so that you're clear about what it takes to get the job done and can articulate it to others.
- Hold a kick off meeting at the start of the project so you can convey the process up front and as clearly as possible.
- If needed, define any terms that your client might not be familiar with.
- Insist that your client appoint one person on their team as your primary point of contact on day-to-day issues. This designee should be able to provide continuity of direction, keep client-side stakeholders informed of competing interests, and give you the guidance needed to make timely decisions.
- Ask questions to gain a deeper understanding of the client's needs. You might find that what they're asking for isn't what they actually need!
- Actively listen to the client's needs without interrupting. We often think of what we might say while they are speaking, therefore opening yourself to the possibility of blocking out pertinent information that should be incorporated into your project plans.

- Restate what you heard the client say so you can leave with meeting with mutual expectations clearly defined.
- Recap your conversation with agreements, timelines, deliverables, and next steps captured in writing.

2. **Educate and inform your clients along the way** – This is perhaps the most time consuming and difficult part of the expectation management process. As the project progresses, proactively communicate with and educate your client along the way.

   Tips for success:

   - Tell your client if a decision they're making might delay your work, increase your scope, or impact the budget or your ability to achieve their goals. Then, give your client the opportunity to reconsider their decision in light of these ramifications.
   - Call them with status updates BEFORE they ask you for one.
   - Talk about changes in the project or process that could likely arise BEFORE they happen and let your client know immediately when they do.
   - Anytime competing priorities or new projects arise that might hinder your ability to complete a project on time, communicate this to your manager to determine how to prioritize.
   - Review your client's expectations as conditions or assumptions change.
   - Tell clients what they need to know, not what they want to hear.
   - Make clients aware of the ramifications of their decisions.
   - Obtain client approval at key points throughout the project.
   - Periodically and proactively make contact with your client.

3. **Set limits** – What happens when the client feels free to call at all hours? Or expects you to turn around a complex job in an unrealistic timeframe? As a professional, it's up to you to manage your time. It is also your obligation to be responsive.

Tips for success:

- Set realistic time frames.
- Push back, but confidently explain way.
- Document, document, document…in other words, CYA (cover yourself!) in the process.
- Leverage technology to manage your calendar and task lists.
- If out of the office, update your auto-response and voice mail messages--note who to contact in your absence and when you will return.

4. **Don't be afraid to "fire the client" if necessary** – What if, despite your best efforts, the client continues to demand more than is realistic? Then it may be time to "fire" the client or walk away from the project. Just make sure you have the necessary support from your boss or the right people who can provide you with the air cover you need before you do so.

You'll only want to consider this step in the most extreme situations and it's not a step you should take without careful consideration. However, many entrepreneurs, particularly those who work in a consulting capacity, recognize that not all business is good business. Sometimes, you will encounter a bad or difficult client who, frankly, isn't worth the money they're paying you. Sometimes, you'll get more from a relationship if you know when to walk away.

In a corporate setting, you'll want to make sure you understand any consequences and exercise sound judgment in knowing when to do so. But, it's an important option that we often forget exists when we're caught up in a performance punishment situation, particularly one induced by a difficult client who isn't your boss.

Tips for success:

- Get air cover from your boss or whoever the right people might be before you decide to walk away.
- Consider outsourcing the project to a subcontractor or outside resource as an alternative.

- Be sure to carefully document what the issues are.
- If all else fails, consider walking away from the project.

5. **Don't over-promise** – Many times we are so eager to please our boss or our clients that we easily fall into the trap of promising too much. The best way to avoid this is to consider that every hour wasted and every mismanaged expectation hurts your reputation as a professional as well as that of your team—and ultimately devalues your contribution to the company.

Tips for success:

- Never make promises that you cannot keep because you think the client wants to hear it.
- Always under-promise and over-deliver.

Managing Client Expectations Self Appraisal

When it comes to managing my clients' expectations, which areas am I strongest in (Setting the Tone, Educate and Inform Along the Way, Setting Limits, Firing the Client, Don't Over Promise)? Be specific.

1.
2.
3.

When it comes to managing my clients' expectations, which areas offer room for improvement (Setting the Tone, Educate and Inform Along the Way, Setting Limits, Firing the Client, Don't Over Promise)? Be specific.

1.
2.
3.

Action Plan – Identify three things you can do now to become and even better manager of your clients' expectations. Be specific.

1.
2.
3.

Practicing Self Advocacy

Ask yourself how you can apply each of the self-advocacy principles to your performance punishment situation. Use the space provided to capture your ideas and strategies.

How can I do better at speaking up for myself in this situation?	
What do I need? How do I ask for it?	
Who else can I engage for help? How?	
What allowances does my company provide to employees to ensure work-life balance (e.g., overtime pay, comp days/flex time, transportation home for employees working after hours, etc.)?	

CHAPTER 12

Strategy #5: Document Your Situation Thoroughly and Be Brave

"The most exciting challenging and significant relationship of all is the one you have with yourself."

Carrie Bradshaw,
*"Sex and The City: An American Girl in Paris:
Part Deux (#6.20)" (2004)*

Although he was the ranking officer of the Enterprise, Captain James Tiberius Kirk wasn't the smartest or strongest person on the ship—that would be Mr. Spock. Scotty knew the ship's inner workings better than Kirk did. Bones was more experienced, older and wiser. And Uhura and Sulu could work the controls better than the Captain ever could.

But, Captain Kirk was a great leader. Why? Because he owned his shortcomings, stood by his team and surrounded himself with others who were strong in areas where he was weak. He also did two things that can help cure performance punishment. First, he regularly took time to document his successes and reflect upon his journey and challenges in his Captain's log. Second, he bravely faced adversity and his fears head on. He wasn't afraid to take a risk and he wasn't afraid to fail.

If you're afflicted by performance punishment, you too must learn to do the same.

Document your situation thoroughly — Since ancient times, leaders have found ways to document their experiences to leave behind proof of their legacy of greatness, to inspire future generations and to teach those who come behind them. If you're in a performance punishment situation, you may have these and other reasons to document your situation.

Our earlier discussion on establishing boundaries and managing expectations touched on the importance of following up to confirm agreements in writing. This keeps the lines of communication open and clear. It also enables you to cover yourself should your client or boss suddenly come down with a case of selective amnesia.

So make a practice of documenting things that you think might come back to haunt you. Don't obsess over these. Just document them and file them away someplace safe just in case you need to refer to them later.

If, for example, a client makes a decision that you think could cause issues later, document your conversation. Be sure to capture how you advised them differently and informed them of the risks involved both verbally and in writing, but the team chose to proceed anyway. This enables you to protect yourself from being thrown under the proverbial bus later and holds the client accountable for their role in what happened.

If you're dealing with performance punishment, it's also important to keep track of your successes. We've seen how being caught in the cycle can sometimes skew our perspective on what's really happening. So it's important to document your wins, no matter how big or how small. Take note of and celebrate the small victories. This does two things for you. First, it gives you a tangible track record you can draw upon in your next performance review discussion. Second, it serves as motivation to keep you going when times get to be challenging. In the process, it helps to reprogram your thinking from focusing on the negatives of your situation to focusing on the positives.

Perhaps the most important things to document if you're in a performance punishment situation are your processes as doing so enables you to help replicate yourself.

Remember that vacation you could never take because only you know what the job requires? If you invest in yourself by taking time to document your work flows and processes, you begin to transfer that knowledge to others. This enables you to act like and be viewed as a leader. It also creates opportunities for others to grow and develop. Most importantly, it presents you with an opportunity to break yourself free of the performance punishment cycle by providing others with a roadmap to learn what you know, so the show can go on while you're away on vacation.

Admittedly, in a world where there's no such thing as complete job security, the pessimistic view to take is that training one's own replacement is either a way to abdicate responsibility, or just plain stupid. However, senior leaders in every successful organization spend time thinking about succession planning and who on the team is next in line for that next leadership role or expanded responsibility. If they view you as someone who is "great at execution but not ready to take on more", they'll never consider you as ready to move on. Conversely, if they see that you have specialized knowledge that you're transferring to others, and thereby helping to build an organizational capability in that area, they'll view you as a leader who's ready to take on a new opportunity to grow. How would you rather be viewed in these succession planning conversations (which, by the way, are taking place whether you realize it or not)?

Oh yeah, did I mention that documenting your processes in order to replicate yourself can also free you up to take a well-deserved break? Moving on then!

Finally, you'll want to document things that you believe are unjust or unfair. But take care not to be ruled by your emotions when you do. Don't document how something made you feel. Only capture the facts. Remember, not everything that feels wrong is illegal. Similarly, not everything that is legal is going to feel right. If you think your situation can only be solved through a formal arbitration or legal proceeding, be careful to focus on documenting facts over feelings. If you should feel deeply in your heart that you might have to plead your case in front of a judge someday, be sure to seek appropriate legal advice and counsel to make sure you're covered. And, as you prepare to make your case, remember that the law doesn't care how you feel about something, and neither does a judge (or your HR department for that matter). They just want the facts that prove the case. So focus on documenting those.

You must also learn to overcome fear — Fear can prevent you from seeing matters as they really are, trusting in your talents, pursuing your passion, establishing healthier boundaries, communicating clearly, recognizing you have options, and moving ahead with your professional life. In other words, fear is among the greatest obstacles you face when it comes to overcoming performance punishment!

Identifying your fear is the first step in the process to overcoming it. What are you afraid of? Are you afraid of speaking up or looking uninformed in a meeting? Losing your job? Getting passed over for a promotion? Are you worried your ideas will not be heard? Or that your request for a day off will not be approved?

It's important to think honestly with yourself about what you're afraid of so you can begin to understand what's holding you back or tripping you up.

Once you've identified your fear, dig deeper and think about where that fear might be coming from. What is your fear caused by? Do you need to work on building your confidence? Do you need access to information? Is a lack of savings or financial security adding to your concerns?

The process of identifying the cause of your fear can be challenging. Sometimes it's obvious. For example, if the last time you spoke up at a meeting didn't go as well as you had planned, or if you routinely observe others getting grilled in group discussions, it's easy to identify that experience as a potential cause of your tendency not to speak up in meetings. Other times fear is more difficult to identify.

Fear is not always rational so finding its source may be complicated. Sometimes the root cause of our fears has nothing to do with anything obvious that we're reacting to. Sometimes it's sub-conscious or difficult to articulate. In those cases, it's helpful to talk to a life coach, career coach, spiritual advisor, or even a therapist to understand what's happening.

Once you've gotten to the cause of your fear, you should rationally weigh the costs of not dealing with it against what you stand to gain by addressing it head on. For most of us, taking steps to deal with our fears offers far more advantages than avoiding, ignoring or otherwise not dealing with them.

For those dealing with a performance punishment situation, the fear of doing anything different or advocating for ourselves can be paralyzing. It can also lead to stress and may of the other symptoms of performance punishment discussed in this book. But, like Captain Kirk, you must be brave enough to face, confront and deal with your fears in order to break the cycle.

In a 2015 *US News and World Report* article entitled, "Overcome Fears to Do Better at Work", author Gail Sheehy offers this advice for overcoming fear in the workplace: "Swap fear for daring."

I'll let you read that again. "Swap fear for daring."

She goes on to say, "To dare risk jumping out of your comfort zone changes the way people respond to you. That changes the way you see yourself. Even when I didn't land on my feet at first – which was often – I learned something useful and dared to try again. The only way out of fear is through."

To overcome fear and performance punishment, you must be brave and address your challenges with the courage of Captain Kirk. And why not? If you're like the Enterprise commander, you'll be armed to do so with the logic and emotional control of Spock, the resolve of Bones, the passion and know-how of Scotty, and the clarity of Uhura.

In other words, you'll have everything you need in order to take full control and chart a new course ahead just like Mr. Sulu.

Documenting Your Journey

- Confirm your conversations, especially agreements and concerns, via email.

- Keep notes of when instances you wish to remember occur using your electronic note pad or calendar.

- Consider keeping a journal. In addition to helping you to document your situation, the journaling process can help you rethink your situation and facilitate self-reflection—critical steps in getting your head straight so you can improve your perspective and your situation.

- Remember, your version of the Captain's log doesn't necessarily need to be written. You can keep an audio or video journal if that's more comfortable or appropriate for your situation!

Facing Your Fear

Ask yourself...	Answer honestly...
What are you afraid of?	
What is it caused by?	
What's the cost of not dealing with your fear?	
What do you stand to gain by dealing with your fear?	

CHAPTER 13

Strategy #6: Chart a New Course

"And so, having disposed of the monster, exit our hero through the front door, stage right, none the worse for his harrowing experience."

Bugs Bunny,
Hair-Raising Hare (1946)

At the end of almost every episode of *Star Trek*, when the conflict of the week was resolved, Captain Kirk would turn to Lt. Hikaru Kato Sulu and issue the command, "Take us ahead Warp factor 2, Mr. Sulu." The ship's helmsman then took control of the Enterprise and did what needed to be done to move the ship out of one adventure and onto the next.

If you suffer from performance punishment, take inspiration from Mr. Sulu, chief helmsman of the Enterprise. Map out a new path for yourself, then plan your work and work your plan to get to where you want and need to go.

As previously mentioned, charting a new course is not necessarily synonymous with finding a new job. The worst thing to do is to change jobs without doing the personal work needed to get ready for a new chapter in your career. Too many times the situations we find ourselves in are the outcome of how we think and behave. So, if you don't engage in some level of self-reflection before you change jobs, you run the risk of winding up in the same situation but with a new employer. And no one wants that for you.

That said, having a good exit strategy and using it IS the ultimate remedy for performance punishment.

Sometimes your exit strategy will mean changing the parameters of your current role using many of the tips and strategies covered in this book. Sometimes, the best exit strategy will be to find a new opportunity within your current organization and other times it might mean switching companies or even careers.

If you can't find a way to reset the paradigm that governs your current situation, then leaving to find another job, career or start your own business may be the best way out. Said another way, sometimes you may have to go to grow.

Either way, map out a new path for yourself, then plan your work and work your plan to get to where you want and need to go.

Remember, you have options! There are many pathways to grow, develop and progress in your career:

- **Up** -- You can move up by earning a promotion or taking a new job functioning at a higher level.
- **Across** -- You can make a lateral move and take on a new position that's on par with where you are, but offers new possibilities.
- **Where You Are** – You can find opportunities by taking on new challenges in your current role or by deepening your knowledge or training in a particular area.
- **New Frontier** – Or, you can boldly go where you've never been before and change careers or move into a brand new area.

If you're not sure where to start, talk to your mentors, coaches and friends who have a sense of who you are and what you have to offer. You should also consider doing some informational interviewing with people in other areas inside your organization, or at other companies, to get a better sense of opportunities outside of your comfort zone. These are two great, productive ways to make your "problem" someone else's as you break free of your performance punishment situation.

Add a career coach to your team. If you don't have an outside career coach, consider finding one. Chances are, if you work for a major corporation, all of the top leaders in your company work with a coach, including your CEO. It's also likely that the company provides coaching to its C-level executives as part of their ongoing development. So what about the rest of us?

The good news is that there are plenty of excellent, highly qualified and affordable career coaches out there and you only need to find one!

The process of finding a career coach begins with knowing what kind of coach you need. Draft a short scope of work that describes your professional situation, why you think you could benefit from an outside coach and the challenge you're trying to overcome. Any decent coach that's worth their hourly fee will start by asking you for this information anyway. So it's best to have some articulation of your needs before you begin your search process.

When I first recognized I was suffering from habitual performance punishment, I knew I needed a different kind of career coach or mentor. As I noted earlier, I recognized I couldn't get to the next level in my corporate career by doing the same thing and using the same tools that I already had.

It took me a bit longer to learn many of the concepts covered in this book because I stumbled through the process of learning them on my own. But one of the many blessings that came out of my journey was that it ultimately connected me with the perfect career coach for me.

Coach Melinda Neissier is a certified life coach who specializes in helping women achieve their goals. Her proprietary Pathway Process was very different from any other career coaching I had experienced in my career. It involved a personality assessment, self-reflection tools, visualization and other techniques that I had never used before. However, when I spoke with her, read the testimonials on her website and learned more about her, something just felt right. I figured I had nothing to lose except for the frustrating situation I was in and gave it a try. And I'm so glad I did.

While she was the perfect coach for me, she was VERY different from the other coaches that came highly recommended by my friends. In interviewing each of these amazing professionals, I realized that each one of my friends' coaches was perfect for them. It was like finding the right partner for a marriage of sorts in that not every coach is for everybody. And that's okay. In picking a coach, finding the one that is right coach for you is what always matters most.

Should you change careers? Hang your own shingle or do something else? If you feel bored, empty or unfulfilled at work, this means you likely are not living your purpose. You might be unhappy at work, going through the motions, being paid enough not to quit, or otherwise caught up in a job because you're doing what is expected of you and not what you were put on this planet to do.

The *Bible* reminds us that each of us is "fearfully and wonderfully made." Each of us was created as a wonder to behold. Bringing forth and sharing our gifts with the world is our responsibility and our mission. It's why we are here. Those who honor their purpose find themselves fulfilled in their careers despite the obstacles and challenges that come their way. It's how two people can be equally qualified on paper to do the same job. Yet one excels and is having the time of their life doing it and the other, well, not so much. Let's say, they're caught up in a cycle of going through the motions every day because they're motivated by their need to chase a paycheck. The difference could be that one of these employees is honoring their gifts and living their purpose more than the other. If you're unclear as to what your purpose is, the right career coach for you may be one who can help you to find it.

Sometimes, our challenge isn't that we're bored, unfulfilled or otherwise unhappy at work. Sometimes we just get an idea that we can't let go of. You know, an idea for how to do something we love, or for fixing a problem that plagues society. And sometimes that idea also has a way for us to make money at it. The thought of working on our idea day and night doesn't matter. "I'll rest when I'm independently wealthy," you think. "Until then, I'm going to press on to bring my vision to life."

If this sounds like you, then becoming an entrepreneur might be an option to explore. The pathway to entrepreneurism is often not a glamorous or easy one. So you must be prepared as entrepreneurial mistakes can be expensive ones. You must also know the business side of the business you're in.

Many entrepreneurs are experts at perfecting the widgets (or products and services) they sell. Where they get tripped up is in not knowing how to take that widget to market, monetize it and run (or ultimately grow) a successful business based on that widget. This is how extremely talented, famous athletes and entertainers sometimes die broke. Or, why brilliant doctors or lawyers may choose not to have their own practice. They excel at their widget (law, medicine, singing, acting, sports or whatever) but they lack the business skills and knowledge needed to run the money-making side of what they do best.

There are many books and articles you can read to determine whether or not switching jobs or making a career change is the right new course to chart for you. There are an equal number of books and articles you can reference to figure out if entrepreneurism might be a path you should explore. In all cases, do your homework. Once you've learned from your coaches, mentors, family members, friends and others who are already on their way to where you think you might want to go, consider one last thing.

What does your gut say? In your heart of hearts, what would you rather be doing? If the world were a perfect place, what would you do for a living? Not to make money, but to make a living!

However you answer that question, pursue that, even if it takes some time traveling down a bumpy road to get there.

If your day job is already enabling you to live your dream, then CONGRATULATIONS! You've achieved what many of us are still working towards. Rock on and continue to enjoy all the happiness you can stand!

If your day job isn't your dream job, then think of it as a temporary means to get there – you know, kind of like a layover in an airport during your journey to that overdue vacation you've been waiting to take!

Use your day job to finance your dreams or to give yourself the time, skills or experiences you need to take a step closer to achieving your goal.

And above all else, never forget that you have options. Even if you can't see them.

Tips for Finding an Outside Career Coach

- Know your objective before you begin.
- Check credentials and coaching accreditation sites.
- Ask friends for referrals.
- Check the coach's website for insight into their coaching approach and philosophy to ensure that it aligns with your beliefs and goals.
- Once you've narrowed your list, ask about their:
  - Training, credentials, experience in dealing with situations like yours
  - Methodology, approach and tools – Are coaching sessions help in person, online, by phone, Skype? Do they use hypnosis, Myers Briggs, meditation, Enneagram assessments or other tools? What's their coaching process, approach and philosophy and what does it entail?
  - Engagements – What is their hourly rate and typical length of engagement?
  - References – Do they have testimonials, references or case studies from other clients they've helped?
- Trust your gut and listen to what your intuition is telling you about this candidate.
- Before you sign on the dotted line, ask yourself and them, "Does it sound like a potential fit?" If you both answer yes, go for it!

Re-claim Your Fame in 15 Minutes A Day

A few years ago, I had dinner with my college roommate. As we caught up on where life's journey had taken each of us, I was reminded of something I promised myself a long time ago.

That is, if I ever found myself in a place where I'm not living my dream, to take 15 minutes each day to work toward it. That could mean watching a webinar or listening to a podcast. Or, taking time to network, informational interview or research a new area. Whatever it is, start with just 15 minutes. You'll find that, as time goes along, 15 minutes will turn to 30 minutes will turn to hours and you'll be amazed at how much you accomplish.

Why?

Because the act of thinking about, then talking about and ultimately being about something begins with that tiny step. It's just like taking that first bite in eating that giant elephant in the room!

No matter how busy we are, we can find 15 minutes to reprogram ourselves to refocus our energy on the thing or things that might really make us happy.

15 minutes is also a small enough interval to wrap our heads and busy schedules around, but long enough to be time well spent if used productively.

Try it.

Set a goal.

Then take 15 minutes each day to work toward it over the next 30 days.

Journal your activity…taking note of how that 15 minutes was spent and what you accomplished in your pursuit.

You'll soon find that 15 minutes will turn to 20 will turn to hours before you know it. You might find that your resume has been updated, you're almost done with that book you've been writing, you've made new connections at your company, have connected with a headhunter with a lead on a new opportunity or that you've even finished your business plan for the company you've been wanting to launch.

Wondering how you'll be able to do all of this in such a short period of time? Because you'll be too busy working on something you love to notice the time.

Tennis great Arthur Ashe eloquently explained this phenomenon better than I ever could when he said, "Success is a journey, not a destination. The doing is often more important than the outcome."

Start the journey toward living your dream by taking 15 minutes to work on it today. Who knows where it might take you!

CHAPTER 14

Strategy #7 - Remember, You're No Redshirt

"Progress. Not perfection."

Robert McCall,
The Equalizer (2014)

In fictional works, the term "redshirt" refers to a stock character who is introduced only to die shortly thereafter. The reference stems from the original *Star Trek* series. A common plot convention of the show involved a sequence in which the characters clad in red shirts were known to die in an episode. Fans of the show didn't always know the names of these crewmen but we know one thing about them for sure – theirs was likely to be a one-way trip to a given planet!

Unlike so many of the hit TV shows of today, it was very safe for us Trekkies to assume with all confidence that none of our favorite characters were going to be killed off in an episode, no matter how dire the situation became. We knew that somehow, some way, they'd work together to use their individual strengths to find a way out, but only after the guys in the red shirts had met their fates.

If you're in a performance punishment situation, you must always remember: You are NO redshirt!

1. While there is no such thing as an indispensable employee – CEOs and even Presidents of countries routinely get replaced – you are talented and capable.
2. Your situation is not permanent, unless you allow it to be.
3. This too shall pass, if you allow it. While you're waiting, use the time to get ready for the wonderful opportunity that lies just around the corner.

4. You can change your entire situation just by changing your perspective.
5. You have it in you to gain control of your emotions so you can see things and think through them more clearly.
6. You can learn to communicate with gravitas, clarity and authority.
7. You have the capacity to persuade others with your passion, credibility and integrity.
8. You are also hereby granted permission to say "no" to others and "yes" to yourself when necessary.
9. You are meant to share the greatness within you with others. So be brave and take time to celebrate the small victories along the way.
10. You are here for a reason so find your purpose and live it – full steam ahead.

Practice these principles every day, especially if you're in a performance punishment situation. It is my sincere hope that they can inspire you to break the performance punishment cycle so you can find happiness at work and boldly go where you've never been before.

All of these principles are within your control. The final section of this book covers a few that you may not be able to control directly, but you may be able to influence inside your organization to minimize its potential for performance punishment to thrive.

Takeaway #3: Breaking the performance punishment cycle is within your control.

SECTION 3

WHAT THE BEST COMPANIES DO TO PREVENT PERFORMANCE PUNISHMENT

CHAPTER 15

Changing the Paradigm

"A true leader does what is right, no matter what others think."
Albus Dumbledore,
Harry Potter and the Goblet of Fire (2005)

The majority of this book is focused on strategies to help free employees who suffer from performance punishment by empowering them to tap into their inner strengths. **My goal for writing this guide is to let people who suffer from that particular affliction know that the power to break the cycle is completely within them.**

But still, I wanted to close with a few reflections on what people who wish to minimize the potential for performance punishment to thrive within their organizations could do to prevent it.

Most companies have employee engagement strategies and partake in some form of listening to employee feedback through various internal communications channels, employee surveys, training programs, or the like. They may also offer competitive salary and bonus packages, vacation time, retirement and pension plans, health care insurance and other benefits and perquisites that employees might expect based on whatever industry and geography they happen to be in.

For the purposes of this discussion, I'm not going to focus on those techniques. While important, they're kind of table stakes, in that every company should have some flavor of them in use in order to attract and retain top talent. In my experience, however, they're not critical to creating a culture where performance punishment can be easily contained.

Instead, I've chosen to focus my closing discussion on some of the not so obvious things that the best companies do to create an environment in which everybody wins.

To start, the best companies create cultures that inspire and empower employees and managers to be leaders, regardless of the positions they hold.

In the simplest of terms, managers have people who work for them. Not everyone is a manager.

Leaders have people who follow them. Everyone has the capacity to be a leader. Some are natural born leaders and others can develop leadership skills along the way.

Leadership is not about titles or positions of authority. It's more concerned with the capacity to motivate and inspire. This is why ineffective heads of state get voted out of office, or in some cases, overthrown. It's also why unsung underdogs can gain great followings and literally change the world.

Consider the *Hunger Games* trilogy by Suzanne Collins. Even if you've never read the books or seen the movies they inspired, you can likely relate to the story: a young girl becomes the reluctant leader of a revolution to free her people from an authoritative, powerful and downright scary leader. She has no official power or authority but becomes a leader of her people by capturing their hearts through her courageous performance in a "kill or be killed" contest. In contrast, the official leader of the land has all the authority but could not lead the people – he, in effect, manages them carefully using a lot of fear and intimidation, but never wins their hearts, nor did he try to.

It's not hard to see how this dynamic has played out in history or our everyday lives. Nelson Mandela, for example, was a great leader long before he ever held an official position of power. And, politics aside, we can all think of political leaders, CEOs or other individuals who held positions of power but could not successfully get the people to follow.

Companies who cultivate leaders minimize their risks for enabling performance punishment because leadership, by its nature, requires empathy, or an understanding of others. Empathy enables people in managerial roles to consider things from their employees' perspective. It also enables employees to consider things from the manager's point of view. In a performance punishment situation, there's often a disconnect between these two perspectives. By cultivating empathetic leadership, companies have the potential to bridge this gap in both directions.

This begins with a clear understanding of a company's mission, vision and values.

Having a clear and widely understood mission, vision and set of values enables a company to:

- Establish the foundation of its culture, which is the true source of sustainable competitive advantage.
- Have a shared rallying point for employees.
- Form the basis of how decisions are made, how the company is run and how employees treat each other and the company's customers.
- Attract and retain the next generation of talent needed to succeed.
- Support the value proposition they offer to customers and channel partners.
- Distinguish itself from the competition by clarifying its identity.
- Contribute to a clear and consistent "reason why" they exist and how they deliver on that reason for being.

In other words, companies that inspire know why they exist and they develop leaders who know and believe it too. They also realize that leading by example isn't enough.

In one of the most compelling TED Talks I've ever watched, Simon Sinik flips that paradigm inside out and encourages viewers to lead by their purpose, or their "why." He explains, your "why" is never about the money. Money is simply an outcome of your "why."

In his TED Talk, "How Great Leaders Inspire Action", Sinik shares some great examples comparing the marketing pitches of companies that start with the "what" (call to action) to those from companies that start with the "why" (reason for being). He goes on to say that the companies who truly distinguish themselves are the ones who are driven by their true purpose, which enables them to connect emotionally with employees and customers – that connection never has anything to do with how they make money.

"People don't buy <u>what</u> you do, they buy <u>why</u> you do it," explains Sinik. He goes on to say, "The goal is to do business with those who believe what you believe."

Since I'm a pop culture junkie of a certain age, let me give you an example to illustrate how this couldn't be truer.

If you've ever seen the beginning of an episode of almost any installment in the *Star Trek* franchise, you know that every show opens with a voiceover that goes something like this…

> *"Space, the final frontier. These are the voyages of the starship Enterprise. Its 5-year mission: to explore strange new worlds, to seek out new life and new civilizations, to boldly go where no man has gone before."*

In three legendary sentences that have been modified slightly through the years, the show clearly established the mission of the characters and for us as viewers as well. Each week, the show runners took care to remind all of us exactly what it was, that what we were about to witness wasn't about gaining more power, money or authority. The show was about what a group of characters would do as the result of being fully committed to their mission. In the process, they got us to follow along faithfully, week after week, year after year, and in some cases, spin off after spin off. They created one of the most successful, lasting entertainment franchises by leading with "why."

The lesson here is to find your organization's "why" and lead with that in all that you do.

The best organizations also rethink their performance management paradigm. Instead of designing a performance review process based on forced rankings, they emphasize developing employee strengths. Areas of improvement are approached as opportunities for managers to develop employees instead of opportunities to punish or criticize them. This involves creating a culture of coaching and intensive development. By definition, this kind of culture is built on a foundation of and belief in continuous learning and feedback.

Research firm Gallup has done extensive research on the impact that this kind of shift in thinking can have on organizational performance. In their 2015 study of more than 1 million individuals working in 50,000 business units in 45 countries, they found that companies that focused on developing employee strengths achieved "business unit performance increases of up to 7% in customer engagement, 15% in employee engagement and 29% in profit." After studying the impact of strengths development for the past 50 years, they now have a dedicated arm of their company that focuses on working with companies to identify employee work styles based on their strengths using the Clifton StrengthsFinder assessment.

It's not difficult to see how developing a performance management system and culture focused on developing strengths makes it difficult for performance punishment to thrive. When employees and managers alike are focusing on the best of themselves, they both win, and so does their organization.

Another item that the best companies are thoughtful about are their work spaces and floor plans. The best companies recognize that office space and workstation configurations can be emotional, and even competitive concepts for their employees. As such, they take care to implement a floor plan approach that is aligned with their company values and business needs. They also take steps to ensure that the context for its implementation is clearly understood by employees. When this doesn't happen, workspaces can be utilized to fuel power plays, performance punishment and other unhealthy dynamics.

Over ten years ago when I first met my husband, he worked in a very traditional corporate setting. He, like many of his co-workers, sat in a cube. And, like many of us who hail from the land of cube-dwellers, he was often interrupted by colleagues who took the lack of physical walls around his workstation as a license to disrupt his workflow at their own discretion. One day, his good friend who sat in a cube not far from his decided she had had enough of what she came to view as disrespectful interruptions. She went to the store and purchased a tension rod typically used to hang shower curtains, along with a regular curtain that matched their office décor. She used these supplies to create a makeshift door for her cubicle that when opened, let people know it was okay to come in for an unplanned discussion and, conversely, when closed, that they needed to come back later.

While I have no idea how this was perceived by others, I remember her saying it was they only effective and productive thing she could think of to do in order to establish boundaries with co-workers who she viewed as disrespectful of her time, privacy and workflow.

I hope it's understood that I'm not recommending this approach, as it might not work in your organization. However, it does raise two key issues for organizations to consider if they want to limit their potential for creating a performance punishment-free culture. First, physical space and floorplans matter. Second, if a company doesn't take steps to create and maintain a healthy company culture, employees will create their own.

And finally, the best companies simply reward the behaviors that they want to see. If you want a company filled with people who practice work-life integration, teamwork and collaboration, incentivize them that way through your policies and total rewards programs. As I write this book, I'm thankful to work for an organization with a CEO who believes in 'rewarding people in the ways that they value'. It's this kind of thinking, backed by corporate actions and policies that demonstrate this belief in action that results in the company's extremely high employee engagement scores year after year.

If you don't know what paying people in ways that are important to them looks like, just ask your employees…they'll be happy to tell you! In some companies, this means allowing people to work from home, in others this could mean gym memberships, break rooms or even on-site yoga classes. The idea is to have a clear employee value proposition that aligns with your company values so you can develop a total rewards program that considers your employees' wants and needs.

Whether or not you manage people or hold an official position of leadership, you can influence your company's culture, which in the end is the sum of what your organization believes and how each person in it behaves based on those principles.

Takeaway #4: Companies that cultivate empathy in their cultures create spaces where it's difficult for performance punishment to thrive.

Self Reflection

What are three things your company could do in the next 12 months to reduce performance punishment?
1.
2.
3.

CONCLUSION

CHAPTER 16

Putting It All Together

"I wish you all the success and happiness you can stand!"

Liz Nolley Tillman

Before you go, take a look back through the notes and resources that you've captured throughout the book. Make a promise to yourself to put them into action and use the worksheet provided to develop a plan of action going forward. Think about what you want to achieve in the next 30 days, 3 months, 6 months and year. Reflect on how you plan to go about it and the resources you will leverage in order to be successful. And, set dates by which you wish to achieve each goal.

You can use your action plan to inspire a vision board, or if you have a vision board, use it to inform your action plan.

Make a copy of your plan and keep it someplace where you will come across it often as a reminder of your pathway out of your performance punishment cycle. And, don't give up!

Remember, you have everything you need to break the performance punishment cycle already within you. Armed with this survival guide and your personalized action plan for some extra support, you can chart your personal pathway to finding happiness and fulfillment at work.

With that, I will leave you with this final parting thought – there's nothing to it but to do it, so get going!

My Action Plan for Breaking the Performance Punishment Cycle

Action Item / Goal (What)	Resources (How)	Target Completion Date (When)
In the next 30 days, I will ….		
In the next 3 months, I will…		
In the next 6 months, I will…		
In the next 12 months, I will…		

ABOUT THE AUTHOR

Liz Nolley Tillman is a marketing communications professional who has spent over 25 years in Corporate America. Liz's experience includes various leadership positions in marketing and communications with UBS Financial Services, Allstate Insurance Company, GfK Custom Research, and AIG as well as on the agency side as a public relations and integrated marketing consultant. As a corporate company spokesperson, she has been featured in a broad range of trade, business and consumer media including NJ101.5 radio, USA Today, Marketing News, Crain's NY Business and others. Her writings have been featured on BlogHer, Work Awesome, Advice4Parenting and other popular blogs. Visit her at www.liznolleytillman.com.

URGENT PLEA!

Thank you for purchasing my book!

I really appreciate all of your feedback and love hearing what you have to say. In order to help make the next version better, please leave me a helpful REVIEW on Amazon by following the QR Code below.

Thanks so much!! ~Liz

https://www.amazon.com/dp/B0731PFXBN/

SELF-PUBLISHING
SCHOOL

NOW IT'S YOUR TURN

Discover the EXACT 3-step blueprint you need to become a bestselling author in 3 months.

Self-Publishing School helped me, and now I want them to help you with this FREE VIDEO SERIES!

Even if you're busy, bad at writing, or don't know where to start, you CAN write a bestseller and build your best life.

With tools and experience across a variety niches and professions, Self-Publishing School is the only resource you need to take your book to the finish line!

DON'T WAIT

Watch this FREE VIDEO SERIES now, and Say "YES" to becoming a bestseller:

https://xe172.isrefer.com/go/sps4fta-vts/bookbrosinc3195

A GIFT BEFORE YOU GO!

UNLOCK THE KEYS TO SUCCESS!

Get proven insights, tips and strategies and find your next career breakthrough.

Download my **FREE Success Strategies Toolkit** offering strategies to advance your career.

- Feeling stuck and underappreciated at work?
- Not sure if a coach is right for you?
- Know what success looks like but aren't sure where to start?

I've got you covered!

To help my readers with actionable insights to take their careers to the next level, I've reached out to three leading career and life coaches to get their best advice and strategies for success. I've put their advice, insights and tips (and a few of my own) into a special toolkit now available FREE to my readers.

Get yours today!

https://www.liznolleytillman.com/secrets-success-toolkit/

Made in the USA
Middletown, DE
02 September 2017